T0293966

INNSBRUCK MOUNTAIN ADVENTURES

About the Author

Originally from Shropshire, Sharon Boscoe spent several years in the French Alps and now lives in Innsbruck with her husband and young daughter. A qualified teacher, she taught in Geneva for many years, and now teaches at the University of Innsbruck. A real outdoor enthusiast, she spends as much time outside as possible, never tiring of exploring the endlessly enjoyable lakes and mountains of Austria. Her love of mountain sports, both summer and winter, has seen her travel far and wide across both Europe and America, always seeking out new and exciting adventures.

INNSBRUCK MOUNTAIN ADVENTURES

SUMMER ROUTES FOR A MULTI-ACTIVITY HOLIDAY AROUND THE CAPITAL OF AUSTRIA'S TIROL

by Sharon Boscoe

JUNIPER HOUSE, MURLEY MOSS,
OXENHOLME ROAD, KENDAL, CUMBRIA LA9 7RL
www.cicerone.co.uk

© Sharon Boscoe 2018
First edition 2018
ISBN: 978 1 85284 958 0

Printed by KHL Printing, Singapore
A catalogue record for this book is available from the British Library.
All photographs are by the author or Charlie Boscoe unless otherwise stated.

Route mapping by Lovell Johns www.lovelljohns.com
Contains OpenStreetMap.org data © OpenStreetMap
contributors, CC-BY-SA. NASA relief data courtesy of ESRI

Updates to this Guide

While every effort is made by our authors to ensure the accuracy of guide-books as they go to print, changes can occur during the lifetime of an edition. Any updates that we know of for this guide will be on the Cicerone website (www.cicerone.co.uk/958/updates), so please check before planning your trip. We also advise that you check information about such things as transport, accommodation and shops locally. Even rights of way can be altered over time.

The route maps in this guide are derived from publicly available data, databases and crowd-sourced data. As such they have not been through the detailed checking procedures that would generally be applied to a published map from an official mapping agency, although naturally we have reviewed them closely in the light of local knowledge as part of the preparation of this guide.

We are always grateful for information about any discrepancies between a guidebook and the facts on the ground, sent by email to updates@cicerone.co.uk or by post to Cicerone, Juniper House, Murley Moss, Oxenholme Road, Kendal, LA9 7RL.

Register your book: To sign up to receive free updates, special offers and GPX files where available, register your book at www.cicerone.co.uk.

Front cover: Moving between rock towers on the Ochsenwand/Schlicker kletter-steig with the Schilck 2000 ski area behind (Route 35)

CONTENTS

Mountain safety

Every mountain walk has its dangers, and those described in this guidebook are no exception. All who walk or climb in the mountains should recognise this and take responsibility for themselves and their companions along the way. The author and publisher have made every effort to ensure that the information contained in this guide was correct when it went to press, but, except for any liability that cannot be excluded by law, they cannot accept responsibility for any loss, injury or inconvenience sustained by any person using this book.

International distress signal *(emergency only)*
Six blasts on a whistle (and flashes with a torch after dark) spaced evenly for one minute, followed by a minute's pause. Repeat until an answer is received. The response is three signals per minute followed by a minute's pause.

Helicopter rescue
The following signals are used to communicate with a helicopter:

Help needed:
raise both arms
above head to
form a 'Y'

Help not needed:
raise one arm
above head, extend
other arm downward

Emergency telephone numbers
The standard European emergency number 112 can be used to call the police, ambulance, fire service or mountain rescue.

The mountain rescue service in Austria is called Bergrettung and the emergency number is 140.

Weather reports
For up-to-date forecasts check www.yr.no or www.bbc.co.uk/weather

Lovely to get off the road for a while and enjoy some peaceful scenery (Route 49)

Symbols used on route maps

〜	route
〜	descent route (via ferratas)
⌒‐‐⌐	alternative route
——	chairlift/cablecar
⸝⸍⸗⸗⸗	tunnel
Ⓢ	start point
Ⓕ	finish point
Ⓢ	alternative start point
Ⓕ	alternative finish point
ⓈⒻ	start/finish point
ⓈⒻ	alternative start/finish point
	glacier
	woodland
	urban areas
	international border
▬■▬	station/railway
▲	peak
†	summit cross
⬆	hut/restaurant
■	building
♦ ⊞	chapel/cemetery
)(	pass
🅿	parking
⊼	picnic area
☀	viewpoint
▲▲	location of crag (sport climbing)
·	other feature

Relief
in metres

3800–4000
3600–3800
3400–3600
3200–3400
3000–3200
2800–3000
2600–2800
2400–2600
2200–2400
2000–2200
1800–2000
1600–1800
1400–1600
1200–1400
1000–1200
800–1000
600–800
400–600
200–400
0–200

Contour lines are drawn at 25m intervals and highlighted at 100m intervals.

Map scales vary: see individual maps.

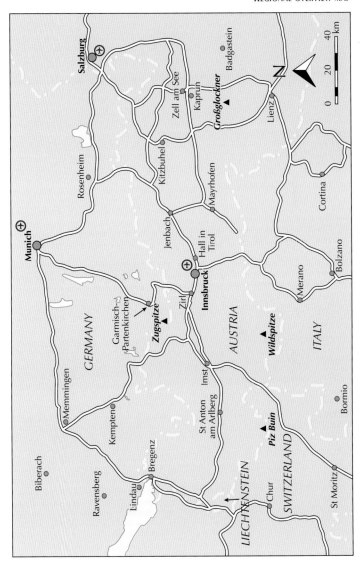

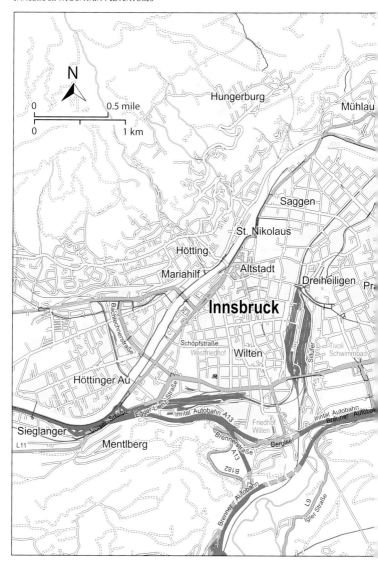

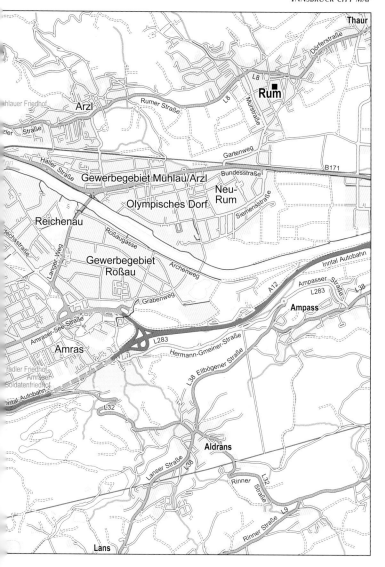

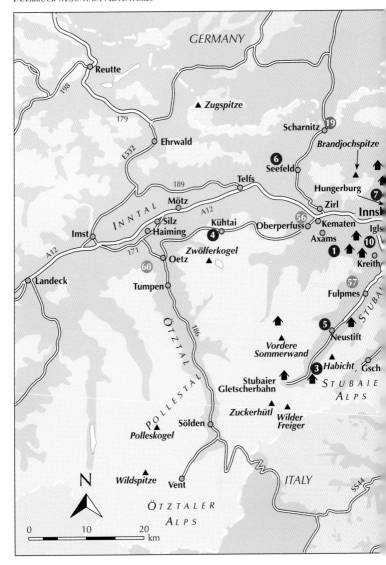

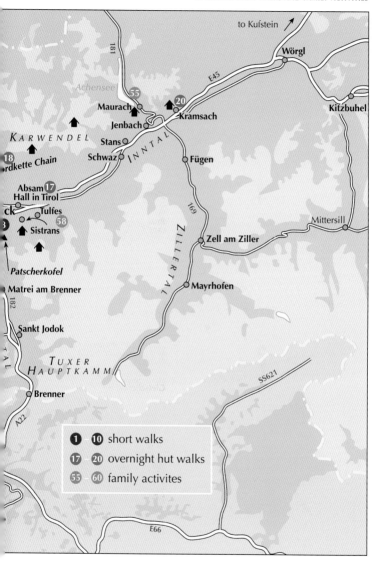

to Kufstein

Wörgl

Achensee

55

Maurach

20

Kramsach

Kitzbuhel

Jenbach

KARWENDEL

Stans

INNTAL

18

rdkette Chain

Schwaz

Fügen

Absam 17

Hall in Tirol

Mittersill

ck

Tulfes

58

ZILLERTAL

169

Sistrans

Zell am Ziller

Patscherkofel

Matrei am Brenner

182

Mayrhofen

Sankt Jodok

TUXER

HAUPTKAMM

SS621

Brenner

A22

1 10	short walks
17 20	overnight hut walks
55 – 60	family activites

E66

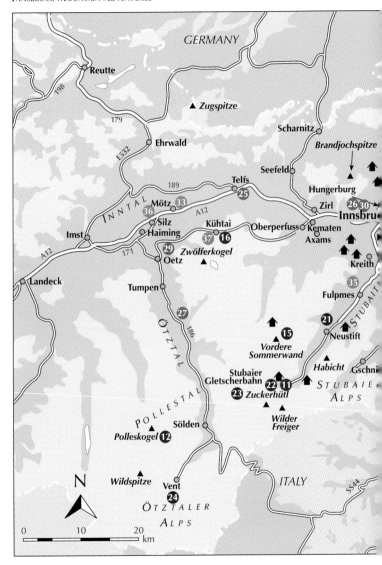

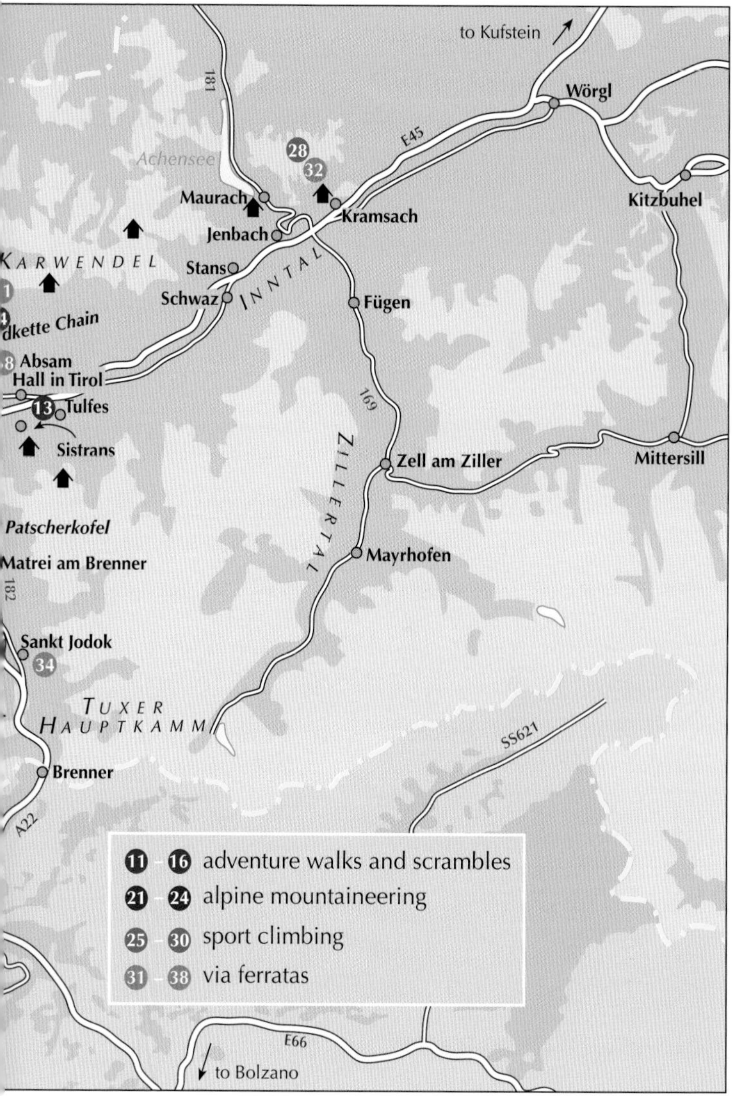
to Kufstein
Wörgl
181
E45
Achensee
28
32
Maurach
Kramsach
Jenbach
Kitzbuhel
KARWENDEL
Stans
INNTAL
Schwaz
Fügen
dkette Chain
Absam
Hall in Tirol
13
Tulfes
169
Sistrans
ZILLERTAL
Zell am Ziller
Mittersill
Patscherkofel
Mayrhofen
Matrei am Brenner
182
Sankt Jodok
34
TUXER
HAUPTKAMM
SS621
Brenner
A22
11 - 16 adventure walks and scrambles
21 - 24 alpine mountaineering
25 - 30 sport climbing
31 - 38 via ferratas
E66
to Bolzano

Happy climbers on the 5 Gipfel (Route 32)

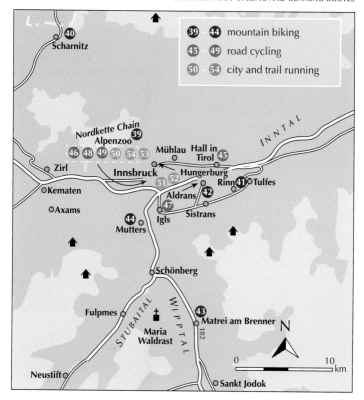

39 **44** mountain biking

45 **49** road cycling

50 – **54** city and trail running

Scharnitz

Nordkette Chain
Alpenzoo

46 **48** **49** **50** **54** **53**

Mühlau

Hall in Tirol **45**

Zirl

Innsbruck

51 **52** Hungerburg

Rinn **41** Tulfes

Kematen

Aldrans **42**

47

Axams

44

Mutters

Igls

Sistrans

Schönberg

Fulpmes

43

Matrei am Brenner

Maria
Waldrast

182

Neustift

Sankt Jodok

INNTAL

STUBAITAL

WIPPTAL

N

0   10
km

Only the train to disturb you on this section of the virtually flat ride (Route 49)

INTRODUCTION

The Nordkette Chain stripped of snow

It is time to consider your next summer holiday. You like the outdoors, you like to try a variety of activities rather than just a single activity trip, but you also enjoy experiencing some culture, some history, perhaps an evening out in a city rather than a small, limited resort. But where in Europe combines a vibrant city with quick access to the mountains? Welcome to Innsbruck.

Bordered by no fewer than eight countries, Austria holds a commanding position in central Europe. With a population of around 130,000 Innsbruck is Austria's fifth largest city and is the capital of the province of Tirol (or Tyrol). It is situated in the west of the country, sandwiched between Germany to the north and Italy to the south, and is just shy of 500km east of the Austrian capital Vienna.

Combining culture, history, stunning scenery and sports galore, Innsbruck can also offer you excellent cuisine, shopping to suit all tastes, vibrant nightlife and a variety of museums.

Innsbruck is fondly known as the 'Capital of the Alps', and understandably so. Its superb geographical location means that Innsbruck is a mere stone's throw from a long list of European hotspots: the Dolomites, Lake Garda, Munich, Graz and Salzburg to name but a few, as well as being in startlingly close proximity to some of the most accessible and picturesque mountains the Alps have to offer. Even a short stay in Innsbruck will leave you wondering how it has managed to stay such a hidden gem rather than swarming with the volume of summer visitors that its Swiss and French counterparts have to cope with. Indeed, this remains somewhat of a mystery. Perhaps it is because it lacks the hallowed 4000m peaks that so many mountaineers strive for, or maybe Innsbruck has simply yet to cross the radars of those looking for mountain adventures, leaving almost all the hiking, biking or running trails around the city peaceful and tranquil, even in the height of summer. Unlike many European alpine resorts, regardless of how busy or crowded the city feels, it is never difficult to escape the crowds and find a quiet forest path.

Innsbruck is probably most famous for playing host to two Winter Olympics, in 1964 and 1976. It was also one of the host cities in the 2008 European Football Championships and it remains a location each year for several sports competitions, both in winter and summer. The city boasts two universities, with a student population of around 30,000, which gives it a young, fresh and exciting vibe. It is also steeped in history with a number of museums and theatres, plus a pedestrianised old town which could rival even the quaintest European cities, complete with cobbled streets and magnificently ornate buildings.

Unlike many other alpine regions, Innsbruck has its own local airport, only a 12-minute bus ride from the city centre. Although not as well served as airports such as Geneva, Lyon or Chambery, several low cost airlines do now fly in and out of Innsbruck from the UK. It is also an easy train or bus ride from Munich international airport, making it a very accessible holiday destination.

Innsbruck's trademark colourful houses on the north side of the River Inn

Innsbruck is a sports enthusiasts' paradise. It has everything that the mountains should offer, from sport climbing to running, and from mountain biking to hiking. For those looking for a varied and interesting holiday, with a wide variety of activities on hand and without too much of a drive to get to them each day, you would be hard pushed to find a better location than Innsbruck. This guide is aimed at precisely those people; whether you are a casual hiker, a biker, a keen runner, a mountaineer, an adrenaline junkie, an energetic family, or are simply content to find a beautiful spot to eat lunch and read a book, there really is something for everyone. The activities are divided into 10 categories, with a carefully chosen selection of the best routes, within an hour's drive of Innsbruck, to suit all levels and abilities.

HISTORY OF THE REGION

As Austria's third largest federal state, Tirol borders the state of Salzburg in the east and Vorarlberg in the west. In the early 15th century, Emperor Maximilian I declared Innsbruck the capital of the region, which it has remained ever since.

As far back as the sixth century, the alpine passes of Tirol provided some of the most important access routes south to Italy, and even today, thanks to the architectural marvel that is the Brenner Pass, it bridges the gap perfectly between northern and southern Europe. Over the centuries, Tirol has been subjected to immense power struggles and ownership has changed hands several times. Bavarian troops took control of Tirol during the Napoleonic wars and changed its name to 'South Bavaria', but it was taken back by the Tiroleans under the leadership of their national hero Andreas Hofer. Sadly, this did not last and Tirol was recaptured. It remained under Bavarian and Italian rule for a further four years until it was finally returned to Austria in 1814. After World War I, the southern part of Tirol was relinquished to Italy. Despite officially being part of Italy, South Tirol is still today largely German speaking.

Tirol was a key battleground in World War I, as the frontline cut right through the Alps, leading to the battles becoming known as 'the war in ice and snow'. Despite minimal involvement in World War II, the conflict still left its mark on Innsbruck, with the city suffering considerable damage and a number of air raids. Following a remarkable history fraught with bloody battles, confrontations and heroic leaders, Innsbruck and its surroundings now thrive as a peaceful hub for tourists, hikers, bikers and climbers, as well as winter sports enthusiasts, living up to its reputation as a sport-loving city.

When exploring the narrow streets in the city centre's old town, the medieval history is ever present, from the impressive Gothic and baroque architecture, to Innsbruck's most famous landmark, the historic Golden Roof (or Goldenes Dachl in German), which was designed as a royal box from where the Emperor could watch events taking place in the square below. The golden roof itself was built around AD1500 in celebration of Emperor Maximilian's second marriage to Bianca Maria Sforza. Today the building houses the International Alpine Convention's Office and the Golden Roof Museum, along with the Innsbruck city archives and registry office, allowing locals to marry in style in the Gothic wedding hall and under the famous golden roof.

Known worldwide as one of the greatest composers in history, Wolfgang Amadeus Mozart is undoubtedly Austria's most famous historical figure. Despite being born in Salzburg in 1756, his legacy can be keenly felt in Innsbruck, which claims one of his childhood homes is in the pedestrian area of the old town.

GEOGRAPHY AND GEOLOGY

Innsbruck lies snugly in the Inn Valley, which is divided by the River Inn, from where the city derives its name ('bridge over the Inn'). It is surrounded on all sides by superb mountain scenery: to the north the impressive Nordkette chain, behind which lies the Karwendel Alpine Park, a protected area boasting the title of the largest nature park in Austria, and,

to the south, the impressive Mount Patscherkofel, which, at 2246m, dominates the skyline above the city.

There are three main peaks which can be seen from Innsbruck, all of which lie to the south of the city. Patscherkofel, with its impressive needle on top, seems to preside over Innsbruck, while Serles (2717m), with its distinctive shape, towers majestically and almost mythically over the southern side of the Inn Valley. The Nockspitze (2404m) stands above the ski resort of Axamer Lizum and is a local favourite for an early morning sunrise hike. A little further afield, the impressively aesthetic Dolomite-esque Kalkkögel Range separates the winter ski resorts of Schlick 2000 and Axamer Lizum.

Unlike many areas in the Alps, the Inn Valley has a number of subsidiary valleys leading out of it, meaning there is a lifetime of exploring available within a relatively short drive, and eliminating the feeling felt in so many alpine resorts of being hemmed in by the imposing mountains. The German word for valley is 'tal', so all the valleys have this as a suffix. The main valley running east to west and in which Innsbruck lies is the Inntal and running south from Innsbruck is the Wipptal, with the impressive Brenner Pass running through it towards Italy. To the west of Innsbruck, the major valleys are the Ötztal and the Stubaital, and to the east of the city lies the Zillertal.

To the east and west of Innsbruck, in the Zillertal and the Ötztal valleys, much of the rock is high-quality granite, providing some classic sport climbing areas. However, the majority of the rock surrounding Innsbruck is limestone with some dolomite, and the landscape is varied and interesting, much of it carved out by the glaciers in the ice age.

Innsbruck and its surrounding areas are largely non-glaciated, making it a great location for relatively stress-free and more accessible mountaineering. However, the nearby Stubai Gletscher at the head of the Stubai Valley is home to no less than 20 spectacular glaciers and has a high point of 3507m, enough to satisfy even the keenest adventurers.

PLANTS AND WILDLIFE

It is estimated that there are no fewer than 43,000 native species of animals in Austria, a vast number for a relatively small, landlocked country. The unique alpine ecosystem in Tirol means that it is well known for its varied and interesting plant life, and the area is also no stranger to wild animals. Innsbruck and its surrounds are probably most famous for their birds of prey, notably the golden eagle, harriers and falcons. Keeping an eye on the sky when out hiking or climbing is highly advised as a lone eagle can often be spotted gracefully circling the peaks.

When driving after dark it is not uncommon to catch a glimpse of a badger or a fox scurrying across the road, and chamois, ibex, deer and less frequently marmots can often be spotted at a distance when hiking along one of Tirol's many mountain

Some of the wildflowers which can be seen along the forest paths; the distinctive Enzian close up

paths. Believe it or not, until 2011 it was reported that a small number of brown bears still lived in Austria, having migrated from neighbouring Slovenia, however it is believed that this tiny population is now no longer, unfortunately most likely due to poaching.

In the summertime, visitors to the mountains around Innsbruck can expect to see several tiny lizards sunbathing on the hot rocks, as well as a huge variety of beautiful, colourful butterflies. Although not strictly wild animals, when out hiking on some of the more remote paths, it is very likely that you will be sharing your path with a herd of cows or flock of sheep, so take care to be respectful and give these animals a wide berth.

If plants are your thing, Austria's national flower is the main one to look out for in the mountains. Thanks to 'The Sound of Music', the Edelweiss is well-known worldwide, with its white petals and yellow centre. Another flower to look out for is the Enzian, or Blue Gentian, which is a stunning, deep-blue trumpet-shaped flower. The Alpine Rose (Alpenrose) is native to the Alps, the Pyrenees and the Jura, and is commonly found above the treeline. The clusters of vivid pink are a form of rhododendron and are easy to spot in the high alpine regions.

For those who would rather cheat and see the best nature has to offer but without the effort, the botanical gardens in the Hötting area of Innsbruck are well worth a visit, as well as being a beautiful peaceful place from which to eat a picnic with a wonderful view. The easiest way to guarantee seeing a number of alpine animals is of course a visit to the Alpenzoo in Innsbruck (see Rainy day activities, below, for more information).

ART AND CULTURE

For those who like to experience some culture on a trip, Innsbruck is sure to satisfy. The Landestheater in the city centre frequently hosts a variety of operas, plays, classical concerts and dance evenings, as well as having extensive and beautiful gardens. The city also boasts a great number of museums, many of them suitable for children and designed to suit all tastes. One of the highlights is the Golden Roof Museum, which is state-of-the-art with touchscreen technology, interactive exhibitions and historic costumes, all recounting the story of Innsbruck's exciting history. It is perfect for children! The Landesmuseum, or Tirolean State Museum, is located just a short walk from the old town and houses a large collection of works of art from all over Tirol. The Tirol Panorama Museum, as well as having some of the best views in the city, focuses on unravelling the mysteries of Tirol, with the help of a giant panoramic painting, which covers approximately 1000 square metres. The Renaissance palace, Schloss

Ambras, is one of Innsbruck's main attractions. Built in the 16th century, it was the residence of Archduke Ferdinand II for more than 30 years. Today it houses an extensive portrait gallery, a rare armour collection and a priceless collection of artwork and late medieval sculptures.

OTHER ACTIVITIES

Other sports activities

As well as the activities included in the guidebook, Innsbruck also offers numerous other activities during the summer months.

- **Bungee jumping** – adrenaline junkies can take the leap from the Europabrücke above the River Sill, which at 192m is Europe's highest bungee bridge.

- **Golf** – there are four golf courses, ranging between nine and 18 holes, within easy reach of Innsbruck, three on the south side of the city near the villages of Igls and Lans, and one to the north, in the village of Seefeld.

- **Indoor climbing** – Innsbruck is no stranger to rock climbing having produced a host of world-class climbers and annually hosting world cup events, so it is no surprise that as of 2017 Innsbruck boasts the largest indoor climbing facility in the world, plus two smaller indoor walls in Innsbruck itself, another in nearby Rum and two further bouldering halls in the neighbouring villages of Axams and Zirl.

- **Paragliding** – on a sunny day the sky above Innsbruck is often

Paragliders getting ready for take-off (Route 5)

filled with parachutes gracefully riding the thermals, and there are numerous companies which will take beginners up for a tandem flight from various take-off points around the area.

- **Rafting and kayaking** – Tirol is an ideal location for whitewater sports due to the clean water, excellent views and suitable rivers making rafting and kayaking immensely popular sports in the summer. There are a number of rafting and kayaking centres in the neighbouring valleys that can organise your whole adventure for you and it is now even possible to take a city rafting trip right through the heart of Innsbruck.

- **Squash and tennis** – there are several tennis and squash centres and clubs around Innsbruck where courts can easily be booked and equipment hired.

- **Summer tobogganing** – this is one of the most enjoyable alpine activities in the summer, and one that can be enjoyed by all ages! Fully strapped-in and secure, you are in control of your speed at all times; a real thrill and a great way to spend an afternoon.

- **Swimming** – Innsbruck and its surrounding villages have several excellent indoor pools which are open all year round, plus a fantastic selection of outdoor pools and swimming lakes open to the public.

Rainy day activities

Despite having a very temperate climate, of course, there will inevitably be days when the weather is not in your favour and venturing into the mountains is not a very tempting option but, fear not, there is a long list of rainy day activities to keep you entertained until the sun reappears.

As well as the numerous museums mentioned in Art and culture, above, Innsbruck also has two mainstream cinemas, the Metropol and the Cineplexx, which show screenings of the movies in the original language, plus the Leokino, a cosy, independent cinema which specialises in showing alternative movies in their original language (subtitled in German, if not German-speaking). There is also a bowling alley, several indoor swimming pools with saunas, fitness centres and a number of wellness centres.

The jewellery giant Swarovski has its headquarters in Wattens, just 18km outside Innsbruck, and in 1995 'Swarovski Crystal Worlds' was opened to celebrate 100 years since the company was founded. The Alpenzoo, although not strictly an indoor activity, is a great wet day option. The zoo holds approximately 2000 animals including lynx, snow hare, ibex, chamois, marmots, beavers, wild boar, bison and a brown bear.

A visit to Innsbruck would not be complete without a visit to the impressive Bergisel ski jump, a real symbol of the city and a reminder of its Olympic history. The stadium, which has a capacity of 28,000, can easily be reached by car, foot or public transport. The site is still used as a training facility as well as a competition venue, and it has even hosted a mass led by Pope John Paul II in 1988 and a number of music concerts. Visitors can enjoy breathtaking views across the city while dining in the restaurant at the top.

SUMMER AND AUTUMN EVENTS

Participants in the Almabtrieb, the end of summer cow festival

Throughout the summer months there is almost always something happening in Innsbruck or in one of its surrounding villages, from free outdoor concerts to traditional live music in the old town, parades of locals dressed in traditional costume and giant outdoor cinema screenings.

- **Summer (Tanzsommer) International Dance Festival** – this spectacular event takes place in mid-June and has become one of the most visited dance festivals in Austria.
- **New Orleans Jazz Festival** – Innsbruck is twinned with New Orleans and this homage to the original festival is generally held in late July
- **Innsbruck Festival of Early Music** – held throughout July and August, this event celebrates traditional music from the Renaissance and baroque eras and takes place across Innsbruck in many of the city's historic locations such as the Imperial Palace and Schloss Ambras.
- **Alpine Folk Music Festival** – continuing throughout September, this event features traditional folk music performances by musicians and singers.
- **Almabtrieb** – this marvellous and colourful tradition, unique to Tirol, is a must-see for visitors to the area in the autumn. All over Tirol, when livestock are ready to return from the high summer pastures, thousands of cattle, sheep, goats and horses are herded back to the valley. Decorated with flamboyant headdresses and giant bells, this is a truly spectacular event not to be missed!

For younger visitors, a fantastic rainy day option is Joy Kids' Paradise in the nearby village of Völs. This is an enormous soft play area for children up to 12 years old, complete with rides, bouncy castles, slides, huge and varied play areas, and a restaurant.

GETTING THERE AND GETTING AROUND

One of Innsbruck's most attractive features, and one which sets it apart from almost all other alpine resorts, is that it has its own airport. Innsbruck Kranebitten is a tiny regional airport, far removed from the hassle and stress of most city airports. There is one terminal and one security gate and, best of all, it is only a 12-minute bus journey from the city centre. However, despite its modest size, Innsbruck is still well served by a number of airlines including Lufthansa, British Airways and EasyJet. If there are no direct flights available into Innsbruck, it is very easy to transfer through a gateway city such as Frankfurt, Dusseldorf or Vienna. Also, do not forget that Munich is only two-and-a-half hours away and Zurich three hours, both with excellent rail and bus links to Innsbruck.

Superb rail connections, low prices and overall Austrian efficiency means that the train is a perfectly feasible and very enjoyable way of getting to Innsbruck. Innsbruck's main station is well linked to major cities

such as Zurich, Salzburg and Munich. The trains are exceptionally punctual, extremely comfortable and run frequently.

If arriving by car it is important to know that you will need a vignette (road tax disc) to travel on Austrian motorways. They are available to buy for periods of 10 days, two months or one year. At the time of writing the cost for a 10-day vignette is €8.90. The Arlberg tunnel to the west and the Brenner Pass to the south also incur extra tolls.

Once in Innsbruck the public transport is second to none, so much so that many locals choose not to have their own car. There is an extensive network of buses and trams which covers the entire city and the surrounding villages, and there is even a regular night-bus service. Tickets can be bought directly from the driver, however, buying in advance from the machines at the bus stops works out marginally cheaper. Innsbruck is purposefully not enormously car-friendly, with bikes being by far the most practical and popular means of getting around. Bikes can be rented at various points around the city, and public transport is often the easiest way of travelling. It is also worth remembering that many of the routes in this book start and finish in different places so leaving a car at the start is not always practical.

See www.ivb.at for the local bus timetables and www.oebb.at for train timetables and prices (both websites can be viewed in German and English).

WHEN TO GO

Innsbruck's landlocked location and altitude means that it enjoys a temperate climate and sees a lot less precipitation than most alpine resorts. With long, hot and generally dry summers and cold, snowy winters, these are the most popular seasons to visit. Spring is generally brief, with winter often blending seamlessly into summer around Easter time, and days averaging around 25°C during July and August. Of course, the temperatures are lower in the high mountains and in early summer the evenings can still be chilly so always come prepared with warmer clothing and wet weather gear regardless of the season. Once the new school year has begun, September and October are not only much quieter but also a lot cheaper in terms of accommodation and travel. With a lower average rainfall than the summer months and temperatures still hovering around the high teens, autumn can be a stunning time of year to visit.

All the activities in this guide are geared towards summer conditions; after the previous winter's snow has melted and before the next year's instalment arrives, so if you are planning to travel outside of high season (July and August) it is worth checking the opening and closing times of the cable cars and chairlifts, as well as hotels and mountain huts, as many of the routes will include these amenities.

Impressive views from the Rofan cable car above Achensee

ACCOMMODATION

Considering the relatively small size of Innsbruck, staying anywhere within the city means you are within walking distance of all the main attractions and amenities. Depending on your requirements and budget, a hotel in the city centre provides maximum convenience with regards to restaurants, shops and buses, however guesthouses, hotels and campsites in one of the surrounding villages may prove a cheaper and more peaceful option. With such a superb public transport network, delightful villages such as Hall in Tirol, Igls and Natters are becoming increasingly popular as a base for holiday-makers.

Camping

The great thing about visiting in summer is that it is possible to camp, which can vastly reduce the cost for those on a budget. The closest campsites are in Kranebitten and in Völs, both an easy bus ride or short bike ride from the city. There are also several camping areas around the very picturesque lake, Natterer See, marginally further out of the city but a beautiful place to stay.

Youth hostels

The cheapest way of staying in the city centre is a youth hostel. There are four hostels: Jugendherberge (www.youth-hostel-innsbruck.at), Youth Hostel Schwedenhaus (www. hostel-innsbruck.com), Nepomuks

(www.nepomuks.at) and Jugend Gästehaus Volkshaus (www.hostel-innsbruck.at). Either in the heart of the old town or within easy walking distance and with prices starting from around €24 per night, they are a convenient and cheap option.

Hotels

A hotel in German is referred to as a *gasthof* or *gasthaus*, meaning guesthouse or inn. Innsbruck has the full range of hotels, from very basic to high-end luxury with wellness centres and pools. Some of these include breakfast in the price whereas others will offer breakfast as an optional extra. An internet search is your best option for finding availability within your budget, or upon arrival the tourist office can help with all kinds of accommodation queries. Be aware Innsbruck is busy in the summer months, and during high season in July and August, it may be difficult to find suitable accommodation, especially if you are wishing to operate on a budget. Book in advance to avoid disappointment.

Self-catering

Airbnb has rocketed in popularity in recent years, and there is a huge variety of choice across Innsbruck city and its surrounding villages. This can be an excellent option for those looking for a self-catered holiday, with private accommodation available in the city centre from as little as £22 per night.

MOUNTAIN HUT ETIQUETTE

Across the European Alps there are some basic rules which are worth adhering to in order to have an enjoyable stay in a mountain hut. Popular huts can get very busy in high season and it is not uncommon for mountain huts to be full to capacity every night. Therefore it is essential to make a reservation beforehand and to try and arrive on time, not only to avoid disappointment but also out of respect for those running the hut so that they have a rough idea of numbers for dinner and breakfast. With regards to eating, make sure you let the hut staff know in advance if you have any special dietary requirements.

Upon arrival remove your outdoor shoes immediately and leave them in the specified entrance area. Most huts provide indoor shoes for guests to borrow or, if not, your socks will be fine. It goes without saying that you should remain considerate to your fellow guests at all times, not least keeping quiet and being respectful after lights out. There is nothing more irritating than being woken up in a communal dormitory by inconsiderate hikers making unnecessary noise and switching lights on after-hours.

It is best to check beforehand whether the hut takes credit or debit cards because many do not, in which case you will need to make sure you are carrying enough cash. Finally, always ensure that you take your own rubbish away with you as you should not expect anyone else to transport your waste down from the high mountains.

Mountain huts

You will be hard pushed to find more comfortable and luxurious mountain huts than those tucked away in the mountains of Austria. Gone are the days of sharing a dorm room with 30 other noisy mountaineers, although this option is still available. In Austria you can book a twin or four-person room at a very reasonable price. Generally owned by either the Austrian (OAV) or German (DAV) Alpine Club, the huts are maintained to a very high standard, the food is superb and there is of course good quality beer on tap! Prices are cheaper if you are a member of the Austrian Alpine Club, and they often fill up fast so book in advance to avoid disappointment. See Appendix B for a list of mountain huts in the region.

TOURIST INFORMATION

The main tourist office in Innsbruck is located on Burggraben, right in the city centre, and there is another smaller office inside Innsbruck train station. See Appendix B for a list of tourist offices in the region. Staff

The Golden Roof shining brightly on the main pedestrian street with Hungerburg mountain station behind

speak several languages, including English, and can help with accommodation, public transport, information on activities and equipment rental, guided tours, activity planning, event and lift tickets, trail maps and activity guides. The dialling code for Austria is 0043 and the currency is the euro.

The Innsbruck Card visitor pass is available to buy for either 24, 48 or 72 hours and covers entry to all of the city's museums and main sights, use of public transport including buses, trams and cable cars in the Innsbruck region, the sightseer bus, Swarovski Crystal Worlds entry ticket and shuttle bus, three hours' bike rental, several of the golf courses and a guided city walk. See www.innsbruck.info/en/ for further details.

With regards to tipping, around 10 per cent is expected in restaurants and bars, however, be aware that the tip is given at the time of paying, rather than leaving the money on the table. For example, if the bill comes to €36.50, it is customary to give €40 and tell your server you do not need the change.

LANGUAGE

The official language in Innsbruck is German, however, the average Austrian's grasp of English is superb and it is spoken fluently by most people you will meet in Austria. Saying this, an attempt at basic German will go a long way to endearing yourselves with the locals, plus it is always fun to give it a go.

Those who learnt basic German in school and feel they can just about scrape by will be completely wrong-footed once they arrive in Austria. If you are expecting to hear *guten tag*, when you meet people on the trails, think again. Austrian German is quite different to the 'Hoch Deutsch' heard in Germany, and the Tyrollean dialect is something different altogether, so do not be disheartened if you understand absolutely nothing! A list of useful words and phrases is included in Appendix C.

HEALTH AND SAFETY

Of course with all mountain activities come risks, ranging from a sprained ankle while hiking, to more serious accidents resulting in broken bones, hospitalisation or even helicopter rescue. It is important to ensure that you have taken all necessary precautions such as checking the up-to-date weather forecast, taking the correct safety equipment for the activity, having a basic first-aid kit and relevant maps, and knowing what to do in an emergency. It is important also to remember that you should only embark on activities which are suitable for your ability, and, if in any doubt, hiring a guide can put your mind at ease.

Insurance

The European Health Insurance Card (EHIC) has now replaced the old E111 and allows access to healthcare across EEA member state countries and Switzerland at a reduced cost. Be aware that in most European countries, the EHIC covers only a certain percentage of the medical bill, which must also be paid at the time and refunded later. Therefore the EHIC card should not be treated as sole holiday insurance; it is strongly advised to seek additional travel insurance.

When taking part in any mountain sports it is always wise to travel with insurance that covers mountain rescue and, in particular, helicopter rescue. Shop around for suitable holiday insurance as there are now a multitude of choices. Some popular options for insurance in Austria are with the Austrian Alpine Club, https://aacuk.org.uk, which has a UK branch, and the British Mountaineering Club, www.thebmc.co.uk, which provides cover for a number of European countries. Both of these include essential mountain rescue and provide annual membership at a very reasonable price. A further frequently used option is Snowcard, www.snowcard.co.uk, where you can choose either a single- or multi-trip option and decide on your level of cover based on the activities you plan to do.

Crossing the gap, don't look down! (Route 35)

35

First aid
All hikers, climbers and cyclists should carry a small, basic first-aid kit. As a minimum this should include:
- Plasters or compeed
- Paracetamol or pain killers
- A small bandage
- Antiseptic cream or wipes
- A small penknife or scissors.

Emergency phone numbers
When calling one of the rescue services be sure to state WHERE you are, WHAT the problem is, WHO is involved and WHEN it happened. Make a note of the following numbers and keep them on you when you are out and about.
- European emergencies – 112
- Alpine rescue – 140
- Police – 133
- Ambulance – 144
- Fire brigade – 122.

MOUNTAIN GUIDES

Guides are not used as frequently in Tirol as in other parts of the Alps, due to the lower altitude and generally non-glaciated and therefore relatively safer terrain. However, there are a number of qualified mountain guides in the area and a guide is recommended for activities such as sport climbing, via ferrata, travelling on glaciated terrain and mountain biking. A guide is especially useful for newcomers to the sport, not only for safety but also to remove the stress of route-finding and planning, therefore vastly enhancing the enjoyment of the day. Guides are locally known as 'Bergführers' and more information can be found at the tourist office or at the office of the Austrian Alpine Club. See also Appendix B.

USING THIS GUIDE

The purpose of this guide is to provide an introduction to the wide range of activities available during a stay in Innsbruck. It is by no means an exhaustive list as to what Innsbruck has to offer, but a selection of some of the best and most well-known options. Innsbruck is a wonderful destination for outdoor enthusiasts, and this book aims to highlight some ideas for those keen to try out a variety of sports, whether you are a couple, a group of friends or travelling as a family. The guide is divided into sections for each activity, with a detailed description at the start of each chapter, along with practical advice on safety, equipment and further information such as maps or further reading.

The activities covered in this guide are:
- Day walks
- Adventure walks and scrambles
- Overnight hut trips
- Alpine mountaineering
- Sport climbing
- Via ferratas
- Mountain biking
- Road cycling
- City and trail running
- Family activities.

The glacial bowl with the Sulzenau Alm ahead (Route 11)

Summary tables of all the routes and activities can be found in Appendix A and a list of routes organised by location can be found in Appendix D.

Grades and timings

The mountain biking and road cycling routes, alpine mountaineering routes, sport climbs and via ferratas are all graded. Details of the grading systems used can be found in the section introductions. Walking and running routes in both the day walks chapter and in the city and trail running section are not graded. They are simply categorised according to distance and altitude gain which will give individuals a good indication as to the level of difficulty.

Rough timings are given for the walking, cycling and mountaineering routes and the via ferratas and family activities. These should be seen as a guideline as time taken to complete such routes varies wildly from person to person. Distance and ascent are also given where applicable and these may prove useful when it comes to estimating how long an activity will take.

Mapping

Overview maps are provided for each of the walking, scrambling, running, mountaineering and cycling routes, however, these maps should be used only for general guidance rather than for detailed route finding. Please note that the maps may vary

The snowy peaks of the Stubaital in the distance (Route 5)

in scale depending on the length and type of route as well as the activity. The appropriate local map to accompany each route is included in the route description and it is highly recommended to take a copy in addition to this guide, especially for longer routes.

WALKING

🚶 DAY WALKS

The start of the Zirbenweg (Route 2)

There are more than 24,000km of marked hiking trails across Tirol. Indeed, the famous long-distance, multi-stage hiking trail – the 'Eagle Walk' – crosses the entire area of Tirol, broken into 33 stages and covering more than 400km.

The network of hiking trails across the area surrounding Innsbruck is vast, varied and superb. From easy and enjoyable family walks, to more strenuous hikes, there is a route to suit all tastes! With spectacular views at every turn, the choice is yours: would you prefer to stay at ground level and start from the city, or make the most of the lift system and enjoy the rewards without the effort? Are you in the mood for crossing alpine pastures, hiking through peaceful forests or stopping for lunch at a pristine alpine lake? Or maybe a combination of all three? Hiking around Innsbruck will not fail to impress.

The mountain huts in Austria are second to none and can literally be found everywhere. Locally known as an *alm* or *hütte*, it is rare to find a hiking trail in the mountains surrounding Innsbruck which does not at some point pass a superb hut. Friendly and welcoming, and always

Elferhütte (Route 5)

with excellent local food, there are so many to choose from that it is a hard task to narrow it down to just a handful. Listed here are a selection of some of the best classic walks visiting the huts around Innsbruck, ranging from short, relatively flat walks to longer, more strenuous half-day walks with more height gain. As every route passes at least one, but often several, mountain huts there is no need to worry about taking lunch!

ROUTE 1

Innsbrucker Almenweg

Start	Mutterer Alm
Finish	Birgitzkopflhaus
Distance	5km
Ascent	450m
Time	2hrs 30mins
Terrain	Hiking trails and 4x4 tracks
High point	2035m
Maps	Kompass Map 36 Innsbruck Brenner or Map 036 Innsbruck und Umgebung
Public transport	Muttereralm can be easily reached using the gondola lift from the village of Mutters. As this hike starts and finishes in different places, the easiest and most enjoyable way to travel is by public transport. Mutters is one of the station stops on the incredibly scenic Stubaitalbahn, direct from Innsbruck train station every hour, taking around 40mins. You must remember to get off at the Nockhofweg/Muttereralmbahn stop, not the Mutters stop. From here the lift station is a 10min walk.

The Innsbrucker Almenweg covers a vast area on the south side of the valley, of which this hike is just a small section. This is a fantastic day out for hikers of all ages, including children, with only 450m of height gain and four mountain huts to break up the day. Mutteralmpark at the top of the gondola is full of fun things to do and will be sure to keep the whole family entertained. There are various routes from Mutterer Alm to Birgitzkopflhaus, however, described here is a lovely route via Götzner Alm (1542m) and Birgitzer Alm (1808m), both of which are well worth a visit. This hike involves very minimal downhill, so for those who would prefer to walk downhill rather than uphill, the entire route could be done in reverse. Just a few minutes' walk uphill from the lift station at Muttereralm is the Panoramasee, an incredibly scenic and peaceful lake with superb mountain views. It is well signposted from the lift and well worth a small detour before you start hiking.

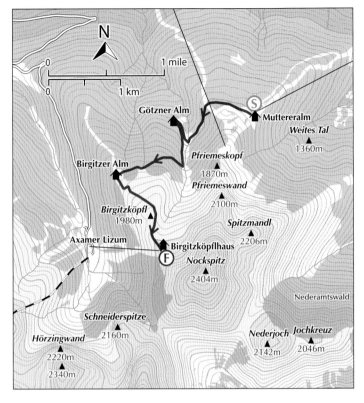

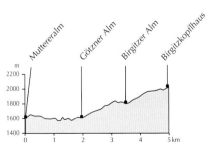

Mutterer Alm (tel 0512 548330, **www.muttereralmpark.at**, open year round) is more mainstream restaurant than mountain hut, but it is very popular and often busy due to its easy access at the top of the cable car, offering superb views and traditional food.

Immediately as you exit the lift station at **Muttereralm** (1608m), pass through the small wooden gate to see several yellow signposts ahead. There are signposts for Innsbrucker Almenweg (in both directions) and Götzner Alm. Follow the path rightwards, heading for Götzner Alm, the first stop on the hike and a 30min walk away. Pay attention to the signs as the path very quickly splits. Continue following signs for Götzner Alm along a 4x4 track through the forest which takes you gradually downhill to the alm itself.

Nestled in a valley, Götzner Alm (tel 0523 432730, **www.goetzneralm.at**, open May until October) is a working alpine dairy farm and produces its own milk, butter and cheese. It boasts easy access, being only a half-hour walk from a cable car.

From **Götzner Alm** follow the signs initially back in the direction you came from, heading for Birgitzer Alm, the next stop. After 200 metres take the path to

Hikers heading down to Birgitzer Alm

the right and, just as you turn, make sure you stay left at the fork to follow the track between the cow shed and the wooden cross. After around 20mins up this fairly steep path you will reach a narrow path on the right leading into the forest, signposted 'Birgitzer Alm'. Follow this forest path, winding slightly uphill and mostly in the shade which can be a great relief on a blistering hot summer's day, for 45mins to reach **Birgitzer Alm**.

Birgitzer Alm (tel 0664 5970026, **www.birgitzer-alm.at**, open May until October and December until March) is one of the best-situated huts in Tirol, with unrivalled mountain views. It is friendly and welcoming with traditional Tirolean food.

Uphill, behind the alm, you will see a sign indicating that your final destination is a 40min walk away. Follow this path and the **Birgitzköpflhaus** will soon appear perched high on the peak above you.

The Birgitzköpflhaus (tel 05234 68100, wildlife.at, open from June until October and December until April) is a delightful little hut with superb views of the surrounding craggy peaks. Located right next to the chairlift, it is a great place to stop, eat lunch and toast the success of your day. From the sundeck you have a wonderful view over to the Axamer Lizum ski area and across to the impressive jagged peaks of the Kalkkögel behind. It is popular with hikers as there are a great number of trails which can be accessed from here.

To return, take the chairlift down to Axamer Lizum and catch a bus back to Innsbruck running every hour, with a quick change in Axams. Make sure you check the bus timetable before you set off or you could have a long wait if you do not time your descent to coincide with a bus.

ROUTE 2

Zirbenweg

Start	Top station of the Patscherkofel cable car, Igls
Finish	Top station (Tulfein) of the Glungezer lift, Tulfes
Distance	7km
Ascent	200m
Time	2hrs 30mins
Terrain	Undulating alpine path
High point	2055m
Maps	Kompass Map 36 Innsbruck Brenner or Map 036 Innsbruck und Umgebung
Public transport	A direct bus from Innsbruck goes to Igls, and regular buses go back from Tulfes to either Igls to collect your car, or directly back to Innsbruck.
Access and parking	From Innsbruck follow Igler Straße until you reach the village of Igls. Turn left onto Hilberstraße and follow this for 500 metres to reach the Patscherkofel lift station. Park here to take the cable car.

This is one of Innsbruck's best-known walks and is one of the sections of the famous Adlerweg (Eagle Walk). And rightly so, it is a non-strenuous but delightful hike with uninterrupted views across Innsbruck and to the Karwendel mountain range behind. The direction described here is the classic route, however, it is also perfectly possible to do the reverse direction, starting from Glungezer and finishing at Patscherkofel, which would be more downhill than up.

As you exit the lift station at the top of the **Patscherkofel cable car** you will see the wooden archway right above the lift station, carved with the words 'Wilkommen am Zirbenweg' leading the way eastwards to the start of the broad path. The entire route is extremely well signposted, with the symbolic yellow Austrian markers pointing you in the right direction at every junction. Continue to follow the signs for Zirbenweg, and after around 1hr 30mins you will reach a fork in the path, indicating that the Zirbenweg continues to the left. Those wishing to extend their hike can also tag the Glungezer peak or alternatively head for the Glungezerhütte

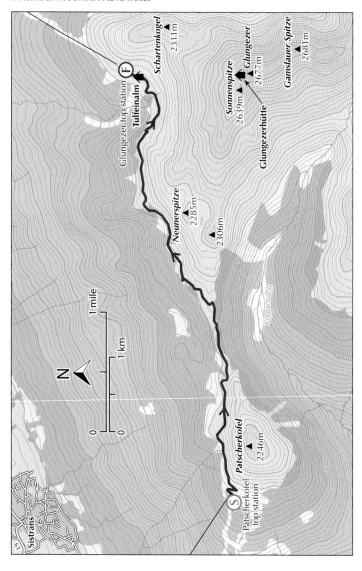

Glungezer top station

F

Schartenkogel
2311m

Tulfeinalm

Sonnenspitze
2639m

Glungezer
2677m

Gamslauer Spitze
2681m

Glungezerhütte

Neunerspitze
2285m

2306m

Vigarbach

1 mile

1 km

N

Patscherkofel
2246m

S

Patscherkofel
top station

Sistrans

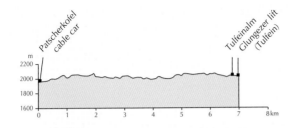

The thoroughly enjoyable one-man chairlift

by taking the right turn here. From this junction the Tulfeinalm is another hour. It is well signposted all the way to the **Tulfeinalm**, a fantastic refreshment stop before the final 5mins to the finishing point at the top of the **Glungezer lift system**.

Tulfein Alm (tel 05223 78153, open December to October) is a very popular hut with hikers completing the Zirbenweg, Innsbruck's most famous hike.

To return, two consecutive chairlifts will take you down, the first being a very quaint and rather unique one-man chairlift, followed by a slightly larger version to take you down to Tulfes.

ROUTE 3

Grawa waterfall

Start/Finish	Tschangelair Alm, Stubaital
Distance	5km
Ascent	190m
Time	1hr 30mins
Terrain	Established hiking paths
High point	1530m
Maps	Kompass Map 36 Innsbruck Brenner or Map 036 Innsbruck und Umgebung or Map 83 Stubaier Alpen
Public transport	There is a direct bus which runs regularly from Innsbruck to the Stubai Glacier which stops right outside the Tschangelair Alm.
Access and parking	From Innsbruck follow the A13 for 10km then take exit 10 to Stubaier Gletscher (toll booth) and keep right at the fork to join the B183. Continue for 24km and shortly after passing through Ranalt and the main parking area signposted for the Wildewasserweg, Tschangelair Alm will be on your right. Park here and the trail begins on the opposite side of the road next to a large wooden sign showing the full route for the Wildewasserweg.

This is a short yet very scenic walk taking in some truly beautiful sights. It forms the first stage of the Wildewasserweg (Wild Water Trail). For those who would like to continue on and make it into a full day hike, turn to Route 11 in Adventure walks and scrambles which describes the second and third sections of the Wildewasserweg classic hike.

The Grawa waterfall in the Stubai Valley boasts the title of the widest waterfall in the eastern Alps at 85 metres wide and 180m high. A truly spectacular sight, and one of Austria's treasures, the short hike is well worth it for the view alone. Now protected as an area of natural beauty, the waterfall is fed by three large glaciers and is said to have enormous health benefits for lung-related issues. The fine spray penetrates the lungs and inhaling it can have a hugely positive effect on colds, asthma and stress. Combined with the proximity to the delightful Grawa Alm restaurant, overall, there are worse places to be!

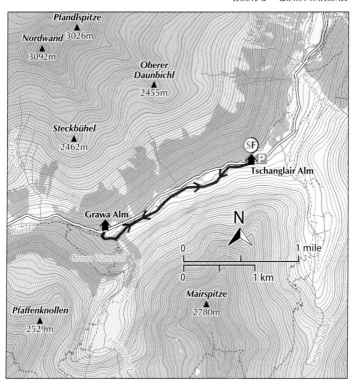

Tschangelair Alm (tel 05226 3767, **https://hoferwirt.at/tschangelair-alm**, open from mid February until December) kicks off the walk.

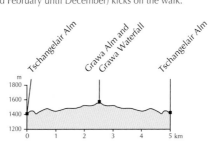

Grawa waterfall from the viewing platform

Follow the signs for the Wildewasserweg and the Grawa waterfall. The pleasant path winds gently uphill following the river, to bring you out at the **Grawa Alm** after a 45min leisurely stroll where you cannot fail to spot the waterfall dominating the landscape.

Grawa Alm (tel 0676 4121009, www. feldhof-tirol.com, summer opening from mid May until the end of September) is an understandably popular hut with easy access directly off the road, and with unrivalled views of the waterfall.

From the terraced area at the bottom of **Grawa waterfall**, it is highly recommended to continue upwards along the wooden walkway for a further 20mins to reach the higher viewing platforms at both the middle and the top. After viewing the waterfall, retrace your steps back to **Tschangelair Alm**.

ROUTE 4

Dreiseen hiking trail

Start/Finish	Alpenrose Hotel, Kühtai
Distance	9.5km
Ascent	350m
Time	3hrs
Terrain	Established hiking trails
High point	2367m
Maps	Kompass Map 35 Imst – Telfs – Kühtai – Mieminger Kette, Map 36 Innsbruck Brenner or Map 036 Innsbruck und Umgebung
Public transport	There is a direct bus from Innsbruck to Kühtai.
Access and parking	Pass straight through the village of Kühtai and drop down the other side to soon see the distinctive pink building of the Alpenrose Hotel on the left behind the Dreiseenbahn chairlift. Park here to begin the walk.

Although a little outside Innsbruck, Kühtai is well worth a visit. At over 2000m it sits on a sunny plateau and is the highest ski resort in Austria. In the summer it is a simply stunning valley, surrounded by imposing peaks with hikes in every direction, some of which can be accessed by using the Dreiseenbahn chairlift. The hike described here, just one of the many on offer, passes several beautiful alpine lakes, including the impressive Finstertaler Reservoir and of course the all-important mountain hut for a refreshment break midway.

Alpenrose Hotel (tel 05239 5205, **www.hotel-alpenrose.eu**, open in winter only).

From the **Alpenrose car park**, set off uphill along the 4x4 track, parallel to the chairlift. This quickly turns into a tarmac road, turn right to cross under the cables of the Dreiseenbahn chairlift. Follow this road for 100 metres to reach a sign directing you left onto the hiking trail, towards the 'Dreiseenhütte'.

51

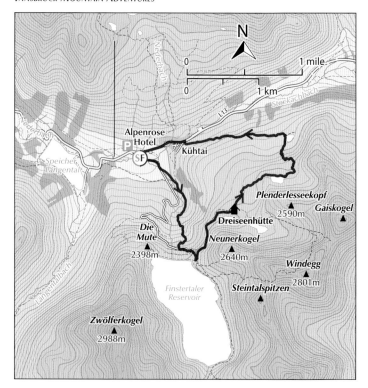

Follow the red and white paint markers as the hiking trail starts to climb gradually, crossing several small streams. Up ahead you will see the impressive dam wall of the Finstertaler Reservoir. After 30mins along this rocky path you will reach a three-way signpost. The Dreiseenhütte is signposted to the left, but ignore this and continue straight ahead in the direction of 'Neunerkogel' and 'Steintalsattel-Pockkogel'. A further 10mins will bring you to a road at the foot of the rather imposing dam wall of the **Finstertaler Reservoir**, turn left along the road and follow it for 50 metres to quickly rejoin the walking trail on the right-hand side, just before the road tunnel. Keep following the red and white paint markers uphill for another 15mins, along the left-hand side of the dam wall, crossing the road several more times to stay on the hiking trail to reach the reservoir itself. Built in the 1970s, the Finstertaler Reservoir and the dam are spectacular feats

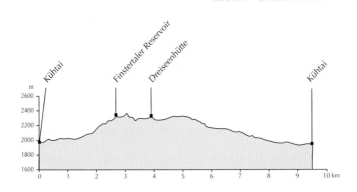

of engineering and provide a superb viewpoint to stop and admire the scenery.
You can walk across the dam wall, looking left over the stunning turquoise blue
water of the reservoir, and right across Kühtai to the ski pistes on the other side
of the valley.

To continue onwards, set off along the 4x4 track that leads upwards and
away from the reservoir. This climbs for about 50 metres then drops into a long,
gentle traversing descent around the hillside. After 20mins you will reach the
Dreiseenhütte.

The last lake before reaching Kühtai

The Dreiseenhütte (tel 05239 5207, open June until September) is a lovely alpine hut with superb views serving traditional Tirolean food.

From the hut initially descend down the 4x4 track but, just after you have crossed under the chairlift cables, leave the road to rejoin the rocky hiking trail on the right. Follow this lovely, undulating path across the hillside through colourful heather and gorse and past a hidden alpine lake for around 30mins to arrive at a fork in the path with the option of continuing uphill to the right, or downhill to the left. Take the left fork to begin a winding descent back towards the village of Kühtai. A further 10mins will bring you to the shores of another beautiful alpine lake. This is a wonderfully peaceful spot for a break, a picnic or a paddle. From here follow the gradually descending hiking path back to **Kühtai** and then to the Alpenrose Hotel.

 ROUTE 5

Elferhütte

Start/Finish	Top station of the Elferbahn gondola, Neustift
Distance	8.2km
Ascent	700m
Time	4hrs
Terrain	Maintained hiking trail
High point	2494m
Maps	Kompass Map 36 Innsbruck Brenner, Map 036 Innsbruck und Umgebung or Map 83 Stubaier Alpen
Public transport	There is a direct bus from Innsbruck which runs regularly to the Stubai ski area, stopping in Neustift.
Access and parking	From the centre of Neustift take the left-hand turning onto Moos, with an easy-to-miss signpost for the Elferbahn. Park here to take the lift.

This is a beautiful circular hike with varied, interesting terrain and spectacular views throughout over the dramatic peaks of the Stubai Valley. Just to top it all off, it then passes the Elferhütte mountain hut near the end of the hike, a great lunch stop and sun trap with wonderful views. There are a few short rocky sections which are a little exposed, where some might be glad of walking poles.

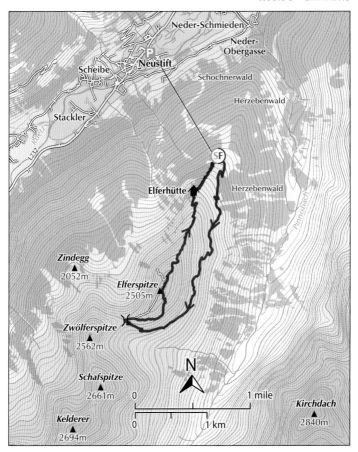

Upon exiting the Elferbahn gondola, take the hiking path eastwards, signposted for Sonnenzeitweg and Rundwanderweg Elfer, to pass the large sundial. After 5mins branch right uphill to continue in the direction of Sonnenzeitweg and Rundwanderweg Elfer.

Wind gradually uphill for 30mins along a hiking path with fantastic mountain views on your left-hand side to reach a flatter section where you will catch your first glimpses of the impressive snowy peaks of the Stubai alpine range. After

55

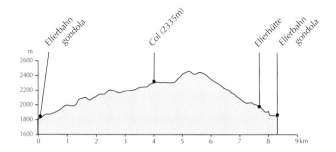

another 10mins you will reach another set of signposts. Stay left in the direction of 'Sonnenzeit', and after a further 30mins, at the next junction, take the right-hand fork towards Zwölfernieder.

As you approach the col, branch right at the junction, signposted 'Elferhütte'. The **col** is a superb viewpoint down to the valleys on either side, and an ideal place to stop for a break. From here head uphill along the path towards the very impressive rock buttresses, also signposted 'Elferhütte'. This is a fairly steep path which traverses around the buttresses. For an interesting alternative, a short grade C via ferrata passes over the top of the rocks, meeting the hiking path again further on, ideal for those who do not mind carrying a bit of extra kit.

Traverse along the rocky path beneath the buttresses, which in places can feel a little exposed, always following the red and white paint markers. After around 45mins you will reach the high point of the hike, signalled by another set of signposts. From here it is possible to add on the summit of the **Elferspitze** with another

You'll need a head for heights on the rocky paths!

15mins climb, or alternatively simply continue onwards downhill in the direction of the Elferhütte, towards the Inn Valley.

From here the descent path is quite steep and a little rocky, and could well be snow covered in autumn. You will very soon be able to see the Elferhütte in front of you, on its impressive perch overlooking the Inn Valley. Follow the red and white paint markers downhill for 1hr 15mins to reach **Elferhütte** itself.

Elferhütte (tel 05226 2818, **www.elferhuette.at**, open June until September) is superbly situated, seemingly teetering over the edge of a mountain. It offers fantastic views across Innsbruck and is a great place to bask in the sunshine.

The final section is an easy 30min walk back down to the lift station where you began.

ROUTE 6

Three lakes, Seefeld Plateau

Start/Finish	Seefeld
Distance	12.3km
Ascent	350m
Time	4hrs
Terrain	Hiking trails and road
High point	1332m
Maps	Kompass Map 36 Innsbruck Brenner or Map 036 Innsbruck und Umgebung
Public transport	A train runs directly from Innsbruck to Seefeld and the start of the walk is a 1km walk through Seefeld village centre.
Access and parking	From Innsbruck follow the A12 west for 12km and take the exit for the B177 Seefeld. Follow this for 9km and turn left signposted 'Seefeld', continue on past the Wildsee Lake on your left for 2km before turning left just after a Shell garage and opposite the Hotel Bergland. After 1km turn left at the T-junction onto Möserer Straße and park at the pay and display parking area next to the tennis courts.

Just 30 minutes' drive from Innsbruck, Seefeld is a quaint, picturesque town with a great deal of charm. With a population of just over 3500, this former farming village turned popular tourist resort is bustling with visitors year-round, and after visiting it is easy to see why. This circular walk is one of many in the area and is a delightful round trip of just over 12km with only very gentle sections of incline. The final two lakes are only 'periodically' water-filled but they provide delightful views nonetheless. And, as with most walks around Innsbruck, there are no fewer than three lovely mountain huts to stop at along the route.

To begin walk east along the main road towards the centre of Seefeld past the Tennishalle building for 250 metres before turning left uphill onto Am Kirchwald, also signposted for Mösern. After 50 metres, at a right-hand bend in the road, follow the yellow sign leftwards towards Mösern.

Continue along a good path for 30mins, following signs for Mösern and ignoring any subsidiary paths, to reach a fork where you should take the right-hand path signposted for Möserersee. This brings you to a cluster of hotels and apartment buildings. Follow the road between these buildings which quickly turns into a lovely forest path, watching out for the yellow walking signs for Möserersee or 'Zum see'. You will soon reach **Möserersee** itself, a beautiful peaceful lake with a walking track all the way around, shaded picnic spots and the obligatory lakeside restaurant. It is also possible to swim in the lake, which is a great option on a hot day.

Möserer Seestuben (tel 05212 4779, **https://seestubn.webnode.at**, open throughout the summer, closed on Mondays) has a stunning location overlooking the lake, and is perfect for a pitstop on a hike or as a destination in itself.

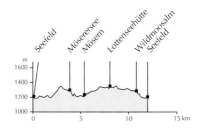

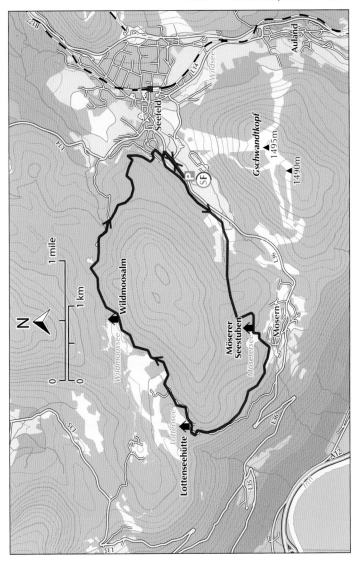

Möserer Seestuben restaurant

Having walked around the lake, head back in the direction you came from to rejoin the path to Mösern. You will quickly reach the quaint hamlet of **Mösern**, from here follow the path signposted for Lottenseehütte and Wildmoos. The path heads into a forest and after 35mins you will emerge from the forest onto a road which leads to the **Lottenseehütte**.

The Lottenseehütte (tel 0664 4003132, www.lottensee.at, open from May until October and December until April) is another traditional Tirolean restaurant which overlooks the periodically dry Lottensee lake.

From Lottensee follow the signs for the Wildmoosalm which starts off along a paved road but soon turns into a lovely forest track. You will emerge out into a beautiful, open area next to the **Wildmoossee**, another periodically dry lake, and the **Wildmoosalm**.

The Wildmoosalm (tel 05212 3066, www.wildmoosalm.com, open December until October) is one of the best mountain restaurants in Tirol, with hearty Austrian food, bags of character and incredibly friendly staff; a fine spot to stop for lunch! It is also a working alpine dairy farm and so a visit is a real experience, with a fun, lively atmosphere, and overlooking a 'periodic lake' that only appears every few years.

From the Wildmoosalm, follow the path which leads through the forest to arrive back into **Seefeld** in around 1hr.

 ROUTE 7

Arzler Alm

Start/Finish	Hungerburg (funicular top station)
Distance	4km
Ascent	210m
Time	50mins
Terrain	Easy hiking trail
High point	1067m
Maps	Kompass Map 36 Innsbruck Brenner or Map 036 Innsbruck und Umgebung
Public transport	Public bus from Innsbruck centre to the Hungerburg cable car station or from Innsbruck centre take the funicular railway up to the Hungerburg station.
Access and parking	It is possible to drive directly up to Hungerburg and park there. A very pleasant extension would be to walk from Innsbruck centre, crossing the river via the wooden footbridge and walking up via the Alpenzoo, which would add just over an hour to the walk.

Arzler Alm is one of Innsbruck's most popular, most accessible and most visited alpine huts, mainly due to its fantastic proximity to the city and easy access thanks to the Hungerburg funicular railway. Friendly staff, fantastic views and a delightful setting all add to the charm of Arzler Alm, which on a sunny day is rarely anything other than busy, but plenty of outdoor seating and a relaxed, lively atmosphere means that the number of people does not detract from the enjoyment.

From the top of the funicular railway, walk across to the far-left corner of the car park behind the cable car station to reach a road (Rosnerweg). Turn right and follow this road for 200 metres then take a small path on the left leading uphill and signposted 'Arzler Alm'. Follow this track for 30mins, ignoring any paths which

Valley views from Arzler Alm

cross it, bearing right and climbing gently throughout. The path enters the forest and climbs a little more steeply near the end to emerge at **Arzler Alm**.

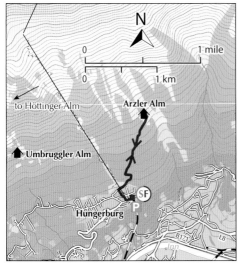

Arzler Alm (tel 0664 6553395, www.arzleralm. at, open January until November) is Innsbruck's most accessible and most popular mountain hut. It is not just hikers and mountain bikers who arrive in droves but also families with children as there is a playground next to the alm, as well as shetland ponies, mountain goats and rabbits. With excellent

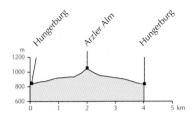

service and traditional food to boot, expect it to be extremely busy on a sunny weekend.

Descend the same way back to the **Hungerburg top station**.

Extensions

Some further easy extensions for those looking for a longer day would be to follow the signs from Arzler Alm and continue to **Höttinger Alm** (an extra 4km with 450m of height gain, allow an extra 1hr 30mins), or to **Umbruggler Alm** (an extra 2.5km with 130m of height gain, allow an extra 40mins).

ROUTE 8

Aldranser Alm

Start/Finish	Sistrans
Distance	10km
Ascent	600m
Time	3hrs
Terrain	4x4 track through forest
High point	1511m
Maps	Kompass Map 36 Innsbruck Brenner or Map 036 Innsbruck und Umgebung
Public transport	A direct bus runs regularly between Innsbruck and Sistrans and stops next to the Raiffeisen bank. From here the start of the walk is just 700 metres away.
Access and parking	After passing through Aldrans and Lans enter Sistrans and turn right just before the Raiffeisen bank. Continue uphill along this narrow road, turning right after 250 metres to follow a sign for Almweg and Sistraner Alm. Follow Almweg until you reach a gravelly car park, also signposted 'Sistraner Alm', and park here.

Aldranser Alm is a delightful, traditional Tirolean alpine hut serving delicious home-cooked food and regional delicacies, with one of the best locations for views across the Innsbruck Valley. The path is almost always quiet, even at a weekend in the middle of summer, and the height gain during the hike is gradual, making it one of the most enjoyable hut hikes in the area. Most of the track up to the hut is completely in the shade of the forest which can be a great relief on a hot day.

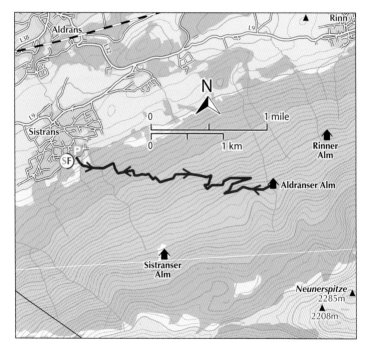

Begin hiking uphill along the 4x4 track out of the car park, following signs for Sistranser Alm along hiking trail number 48. Stay on this wide 4x4 track which winds its way gently upwards through the forest, ignoring any subsidiary roads. After around 40mins you will see a sign for Aldranser Alm and a gap in the trees opens up to reveal a beautiful view of the Inn Valley. Ten minutes further on you

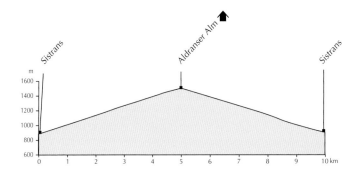

will come to a junction with Aldranser Alm signposted to the left, along hiking trail number 47. Take this path, which quickly becomes narrower and soon opens up to reveal stunning views of the Nordkette mountain chain. This narrower section then rejoins another established 4x4 track and is signposted for Aldranser

Great views from Aldranser Alm

Alm. Continue following this main track to reach a left-hand turn, again clearly signposted towards **Aldranser Alm**, which leads downhill to the alm itself.

> Aldranser Alm (tel 0664 1516675, **www.aldranseralm.at**, open May until October, closed on Thursdays), in addition to offering traditional, hearty Tirolean food and fantastic views across the valley, also hosts a great deal of evening entertainment, including jazz nights and live music. It is an alpine hut with a difference and well worth a visit during the day or at night!

Descend back to **Sistrans** via the same route.

Extensions

To extend the day it is also possible to continue to both the **Rinner Alm** or the **Sistranser Alm**, both of which are around 30mins' hike from Aldranser Alm, and are signposted from the final junction. From Sistranser Alm you can take a slightly different descent route, following the signs back down to Sistrans, which takes about 1hr 30mins; and from Rinner Alm you have the option of either returning the way you came or following the hiking trail from Rinner Alm down to village of Rinn which takes around 1hr, from where there are regular buses back to Innsbruck or Sistrans.

 ROUTE 9

Bodenstein Alm

Start/Finish	Hungerburg (funicular top station)
Distance	14km
Ascent	800m
Time	4hrs
Terrain	Well-maintained hiking trails
High point	1661m
Maps	Kompass Map 36 Innsbruck Brenner or Map 036 Innsbruck und Umgebung
Public transport	Public bus from Innsbruck centre to the Hungerburg cable car station or from Innsbruck centre take the funicular railway up to the Hungerburg station.
Access and parking	It is possible to drive up to Hungerburg and park there.

Hidden at the end of a short trail, and off the beaten track, the Bodenstein Alm is not as crowded as some of the other mountain huts around Innsbruck. Serving traditional Austrian food and good beer, many mountain bikers choose to take a break here on their tour from either Arzler Alm or Höttinger Alm and it is also a great pit stop for hikers on their way up or down, providing a more relaxed and authentic alternative to the bustling restaurant at Seegrube cable car station.

There are several routes up to Bodenstein Alm. The one you choose will depend on whether you would like a gentle, more gradual climb, or a steeper, more direct route providing more of a physical workout. The routes all converge at some point, and as long as you are always heading uphill and roughly following the cables overhead it is fairly difficult to get lost. Be aware that if you take the well-established 4x4 track up to the alm, you will be sharing it with mountain bikers travelling both up and down, often at great speed!

Walk across to the far-left corner of the car park behind the cable car station to reach a road (Rosnerweg). The easiest and most enjoyable route goes via Arzler Alm, which initially seems to be taking you in the wrong direction and does make the hike longer but it avoids the steep slog which is the more direct route. To take this route, follow the directions up to **Arzler Alm** (see Route 7) and from here turn left on the wide 4x4 track that runs directly in front of the alm. See below for the steeper, more direct route.

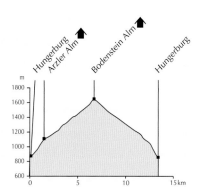

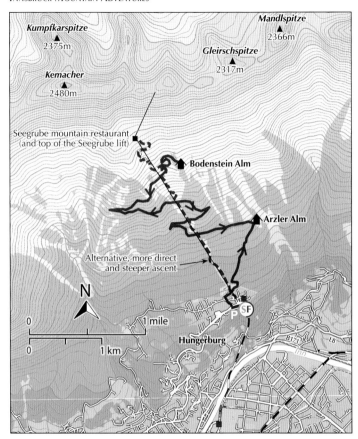

From Arzler Alm this 4x4 track leads all the way to the top of the Seegrube lift, which is the mid-station of the Nordkette cable car and sits just 300m higher than the Bodenstein Alm. It is signs for Bodensteinalm, along hiking trail 216 that you should continue following throughout the hike. The 4x4 track is the most pleasant route up to Bodenstein Alm, winding gently in and out of the forest, however, there are occasionally smaller paths signposted for Seegrube which cut the wide sweeping corners of the 4x4 track. These provide a shortcut, albeit a little steeper, and eventually emerge to rejoin the track. After just over 2hrs of walking you will round a corner to see, along the track ahead of you, the bottom of a chairlift. Just as this comes into view (at altitude 1650m) there is a significant track leading off to the right, clearly signposted for **Bodenstein Alm**. Follow this track for 5mins to reach the alm.

> Bodenstein Alm (tel 0664 1043945, open May until October) is a traditional Tirolean hut with excellent views across the Inn Valley.

Alternative route
The alternative, more direct and steeper route also starts from Rosnerweg, the road behind the car park in Hungerburg, yet rather than turning onto the road, cross directly over it to follow a very well-marked gravel path leading uphill and signposted 'Seegrube (Seilbahnsteig) 3hrs' at the bottom. Follow this path, which soon turns into a grassy forest track, pass a children's play area and join a narrow path which follows the line of the cables overhead and heads steeply uphill. At the top of this steep uphill section, continue following signs for 'Seegrube (Seilbahnsteig)' to eventually rejoin the main track.

Descend the same way you came up.

Mountain huts are always well taken care of in Austria and flowers play a big part

Alternative descent (Seegrube lift)

Alternatively, you can rejoin the main 4x4 track leading from Hungerburg and continue upwards for a further 1hr to reach the Seegrube mountain station. From here it is possible to take the cable car directly back down to the Hungerburg station.

 ROUTE 10

Kreither Alm

Start/Finish	Kreith
Distance	8km
Ascent	490m
Time	3hrs
Terrain	4x4 track/hiking path
High point	1492m
Maps	Kompass Map 36 Innsbruck Brenner or Map 036 Innsbruck und Umgebung
Public transport	The Stubaitalbahn tram (STB) leaves regularly from Innsbruck train station and takes around 40mins to reach Kreith. This scenic journey is by far the easiest, simplest and most enjoyable way of travelling as it takes you directly to the centre of Kreith and the start of the walk.
Access and parking	On reaching Kreith, drive straight through the village passing the tram stop on the left (which is where you should alight if you took the tram) and continue uphill passing a yellow hiking sign for Kreither Alm, to reach a parking area with space for around 15 cars, directly on a 180-degree bend in the road. There is also additional parking on the road.

The gentle hike to Kreither Alm, a family run alpine hut at the foot of the impressive Nockspitze, rewards with magnificent views of the Inn Valley and across to the Patscherkofel peak. You can descend the way you came, but this route takes a circular option passing the lovely Alpengasthaus Stockerhof on the way back.

This hiking trail is also part of the popular Kreitheralmweg which is a mountain bike route, so be aware that you may be sharing the path with cyclists.

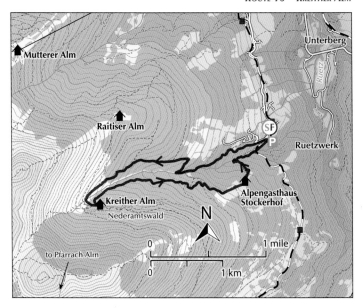

From the parking area start walking along the 4x4 track uphill, where a signpost indicates you are 1hr 30mins away from Kreither Alm. After 30mins keep right at the fork, following the wooden sign directing you towards Kreither Alm. This track winds uphill through the forest with signs for the alm at every junction, eventually bringing you out at **Kreither Alm** itself.

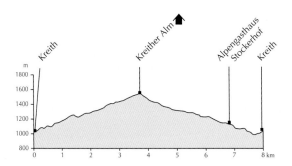

Friendly and welcoming Kreither Alm

Tucked away along a forest trail, Kreither Alm (tel 0677 61669613, **www. kreither-alm.at**, open early June until mid October) is a delightful place to stop for lunch or a drink. Friendly, traditional and with the standard lovely views, it is very popular with mountain bikers and hikers.

To descend, take the path onwards from Kreither Alm, rather than back the way you just arrived, signposted 'Pfarrach Alm' (which is a lovely addition to the walk for those who wish to extend the day further). The narrow forest path soon rejoins a wide 4x4 track, signposted 'Stockerhof 40m'. Continue down this track, at every junction following the signs for 'Stockerhof', to reach the the beautifully situated **Alpengasthaus Stockerhof**.

Alpengasthaus Stockerhof (tel 0664 5328806, open daily throughout the summer) is situated on a wide, sunny plateau with fantastic views.

From here the final section follows a slightly steeper path through the forest and brings you back to the tram stop in **Kreith**.

Extensions
There are some options to extend this route. It would take around 1hr 15mins of gentle, undulating hiking along a forest track to reach **Mutterer Alm** from Kreither Alm, via **Raitiser Alm**. From Mutterer Alm it is possible to take a cable car down

Popular with both bikers and hikers

to the village of Mutters, from where there is easy public transport back to either Innsbruck or Kreith. The path to Pfarrach Alm follows a gradual uphill to begin with then undulates gently for the second half, roughly following the contour. Allow 1hr 30mins. From the Pfarrach Alm, a descent of around 1hr 45 mins will bring you to the village of Telfes, where there is a regular tram to take you back to either Kreith or Innsbruck.

🧍 ADVENTURE WALKS AND SCRAMBLES

Nearing the summit of Vordere Sommerwand (Route 15)

This section is for the more adventurous outdoor enthusiast, with the routes not needing quite as much expertise or equipment as is required for mountaineering or rock climbing. The routes bridge the gap between hiking and mountaineering, and although most may require the occasional use of a rope, the grade is never more difficult than scrambling grade 3, rendering it scrambling rather than climbing. The rope could well stay in your bag from start to finish, but it is always better to have it and not use it than decide not to bring it and find yourself stuck. Some of the routes are simply longer, more strenuous hikes, occasionally needing to use cables or chains, which makes them feel much more adventurous and exciting than a standard hike. Many of the routes are classic ridge scrambles, with spectacular views throughout and finishing at a thoroughly rewarding summit. Make sure you check the information boxes at the start of the route descriptions under 'Equipment' for what gear is necessary before setting off to avoid running into any unexpected problems.

Adventure walks and scrambles are graded from 1 to 3 according to the British Mountaineering Council's grading system, with 1 being essentially a slightly more adventurous and possibly exposed hike, with no climbing skills needed, through to 3 which is a moderately graded climb, including sections with may require a rope.

ROUTE 11
Wildewasserweg

Start/Finish	Grawa Alm
Distance	14km
Ascent	1060m
Grade	n/a (no technical difficulty so no grading, but classed as an adventure hike because it is long and strenuous)
Time	6hrs 30mins
Terrain	Wooden walkways, hiking paths, some rocky steps
High point	2540m
Maps	Kompass Map 36 Innsbruck Brenner, Map 036 Innsbruck und Umgebung or Map 83 Stubaier Alpen
Public transport	There is a direct bus from Innsbruck which runs regularly to the Stubai ski area and stops at the Grawa Alm.
Access and parking	From Innsbruck follow the A13 for 10km then take exit 10 to Stubaier Gletscher (toll booth) and keep right at the fork to join the B183. Continue on this road for 26km and shortly after passing through Ranalt, continue on past the main parking area for the Wildewasserweg and Tschangelair Alm to reach the Grawa Waterfall itself on the left. Parking is on the right-hand side of the road, opposite the Grawa Alm and next to the huge sign for Wildewasserweg.

The Wildewasserweg (Wild Water Trail) in the Stubai Valley is one of Tirol's classic hikes and could not come more highly recommended. Passing through a huge variety of landscapes from waterfalls and forests to glacial basins and mountain lakes, this superb adventure hike is broken up into three clear stages, meaning that you can choose to complete just one, two or all three.

The first stage of the hike, Tschangelair Alm to Grawa Waterfall, is covered in Route 3. The second and third stages of the hike are described here from the Grawa Alm to the Sulzenauferner Glacier.

STAGE BREAKDOWN
Stage 1 Tschangelair Alm–Grawa Alm: 45mins, 190m, 2.5km
Stage 2 Grawa Alm –Sulzenau Alm and Sulzenauhütte: 2hrs, 660m, 4km
Stage 3 Sulzenauhütte–Sulzenauferner Glacier: 1hr 20mins, 400m, 3km

Grawa Alm (tel 0676 4121009, **www.feldhof-tirol.com**, summer opening from mid May until end of September) is an understandably popular hut with easy access directly off the road, and with unrivalled views of the Grawa Waterfall.

Walk around to the right-hand side of the Grawa Alm, to cross the river and make the short 5min journey to the waterfall itself. It is well worth spending some time here on the terrace, soaking up some of the healing spray from the waterfall, which is said to have positive health benefits on the upper respiratory tract and significantly improve breathing-related health problems.

From here follow the wooden walkway uphill through the forest on the right-hand side of the waterfall, signposted for the Sulzenau Alm and Sulzenauhütte, past two further viewing platforms. After around 50mins you will emerge out above the trees to a beautiful view of the glacier high above. Here the path flattens out into a large glacial bowl, with the **Sulzenau Alm** and another fantastic waterfall up ahead.

Looking back down the glacial bowl to the Sulzenau Alm

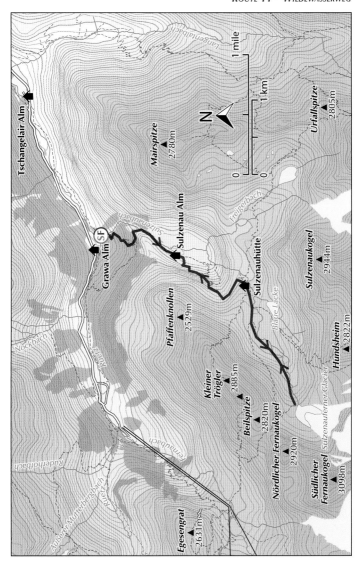

The following map labels appear:

Langentalbach

Tschangelair Alm

Mairspitze 2780m

Urfallspitze 2805m

N

1 mile

1 km

0

Freigerbach

Sulzenau Alm

Sulzenaubach

SF

Grawa Alm

Sulzenauhütte

Sulzenaukogel 2944m

Pfaffenknollen 2529m

Blaue Lacke

Hundsheim 2822m

Nockbach

Ruetz

Kleiner Trögler 2885m

Beilspitze 2820m

Nördlicher Fernaukogel 2920m

Sulzenauferner Glacier

Fernaubach

Südlicher Fernaukogel 3098m

Rudelhofbach

Alperer Mutterbergbach

Ruetz

Egesengrat 2631m

The Sulzenau Alm (tel 0676 5603090, **www.sulzenau-alm.at**, open from May until October) provides rather idyllic views and a perfect place to stop for a break before continuing upwards.

High up ahead you can now see the next stop on the route, the Sulzenauhütte, teetering precariously at the top of the waterfall. From the alm, cross the glacial bowl towards the waterfall to reach a sign indicating that the Sulzenauhütte can be reached by following either direction. Both paths merge later on and lead to the hut so it does not matter which one you choose. Follow the path winding upwards for another 45mins to reach **Sulzenauhütte** sitting on an impressive plateau.

Sulzenauhütte (tel 0664 2716898, **www.sulzenauhuette.at**, open early June until end of September), run by the same family for four generations, is a perfect sun trap and one of the main bases for mountain activities in the Stubai Alps.

The final stage of the walk continues on behind the hut, following the river and the direction of the Wilderwasserweg, heading towards the glacier. The river becomes increasingly wilder and the path more rocky but it is easy to follow with red and white paint markers throughout. After 10mins it is well worth taking the short detour to the **Blaue Lacke**, a beautiful lake surrounded by hundreds of cairns. After a final 50mins there is a short steep climb which brings you out at the end of the Wilderwasserweg and a spectacular glacial lake at the foot of the **Sulzenauferner Glacier** which towers above.

To descend, reverse your route back down via the Sulzenauhütte, the Sulzenau Alm and the **Grawa Alm**.

Blaue Lacke complete with cairns

ROUTE 12
*Südlicher and
Nordlicher Polleskogel*

Start/Finish	Tiefenbachgletscher parking area, Ötztaler Gletscherstrasse
Ascent	225m
Grade	1–2
Time	2–3hrs
Terrain	Hiking trails and ridge scrambling, small sections of easy via ferrata
High point	3035m
Maps	Kompass Map 43 Ötztaler Alpen – Ötztal – Pitztal
Public transport	Take the train from Innsbruck to Ötztal, then a bus from Ötztal to Sölden. From Sölden take a bus up to the Gletscherstraße.
Access and parking	Drive through Sölden to reach the Gaislachkogelbahn cable car. Continue south on the B186 for 900 metres to a large green sign directing you right to 'Rettenbachgletscher 12km' and 'Tiefenbachgletscher 14km'. Take this right-hand turning and follow the road uphill for 500 metres to a junction where another green sign for 'Gletscher' sends you left. You are now on the famous Gletscherstraße (Glacier Road). Follow it through stunning scenery for 11.5km to the Rettenbachgletscher parking area at 2675m. Take in the view and then continue for 2km more to reach Tiefenbachgletscher parking area at 2800m. Snowfall is possible here even in summer – do not get caught up here in bad weather as getting a car back down the Gletscherstraße in snowy conditions would be extremely treacherous! Park at the Tiefenbachgletscher parking area. Bear in mind with a toll of €20 to drive up the Gletscherstraße, the bus from Sölden could be a cheaper option.
Equipment	Harness, via ferrata lanyards, helmet

The Polleskogel peaks in the Ötztal Alps are two of the most popular and easiest 3000m peaks in Tirol due to their easy access from the Ötztaler Gletscherstrasse (Glacier Road), meaning the climb starts at 2800m. The Northern (Nordlicher) and Southern (Südlicher) peaks, at 3015m and 3035m respectively, are mainly scrambles with a few small sections of via ferrata. From the end of the Ötztaler Gletscherstrasse the ascent is between one and one and a half hours. It is possible to climb both peaks in the same day by descending back to the ridge after summiting and this time follow it to the north. Overall this is a brilliant 'half day hit' which allows you to climb two 3000m peaks in a two-hour round trip, with wonderful views throughout! The route can extended by parking in Längenfeld and descending via the wonderful Pollestal Valley.

Walk north west following a path as well as red and white paint marks on the rocks. The path leads up and right to the foot of a rock buttress with '911' painted in red at the bottom. Just 20 metres higher up, on the right of the buttress, '911' is

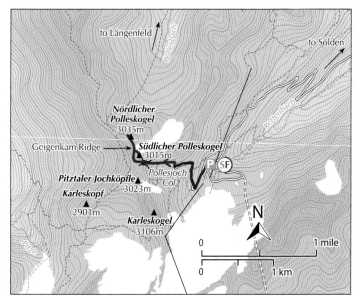

Ascent is also possible in the winter!

painted again, this time in red and white. This second painted sign marks the start of a series of metal chains which protect the next section. Reaching here takes 20mins from the Tiefenbachgletscher parking area.

Follow the chains for 10mins up some easy but occasionally exposed terrain to reach a col, the **Pollesjoch**. Most experienced scramblers will not require any protection during the chain section, but those not keen on exposure might be glad of a harness and via ferrata lanyards to clip in with. From the Pollesjoch, make a 20m descending traverse on a good path to the start of some more chains where the path begins to go uphill. Follow the chains and the path for 5mins to the **Geigenkam Ridge** which separates the two Polleskogel summits. The **Südlicher Polleskogel** is on the right and the summit is reached via a 5min scramble. The scramble is quite straightforward (grade 1–2) but is quite exposed and there is no protection so a bit of scrambling experience is vital. From the summit the view across the glaciers of Sölden ski area is wonderful.

Descend back to where the path and chains reached the ridge and continue northwards along the Geigenkam Ridge via a good path. The **Nördlicher Polleskogel** is reached after 10mins of easy walking. (It is of course possible to skip out the Südlicher Polleskogel and just go directly to the Nordlicher from the top of the chains.)

To descend, retrace the ascent route back to the Tiefenbachgletscher parking area.

Extension to Längenfeld

A good option for those looking to turn these peaks into a full day out is to park in the village of Längenfeld then take a bus to Sölden, followed by another bus up the Gletscherstraße. Climb the two peaks and then, from the summit of the Nordlicher Polleskogel, continue north along the Geigenkam Ridge for 200 metres to a path leading off right, into the Pollestal Valley. Follow the path down the valley, which is wild and beautiful, for 4hrs to reach Längenfeld.

ROUTE 13

Glungezer klettersteig

Start/Finish	Top station (Tulfein) of the Glungezer lift, Tulfes
Ascent	550m
Grade	2
Time	3hrs 30mins
Terrain	Hiking trails, easy scrambling and very short sections of via ferrata
High point	2610m
Maps	Kompass Map 36 Innsbruck Brenner or Map 036 Innsbruck und Umgebung
Public transport	A direct bus will take you from Innsbruck to Tulfes in just over 30mins. See below for chairlift information.
Access and parking	Upon reaching Tulfes, pass through the village and follow the signs for 'Glungezerbahn' (lift station) where there is ample parking. From the lift station, take the two-man chairlift (a 20min ride), then walk downhill to a one-man chairlift (another 20min ride).
Equipment	Harness, via ferrata lanyards, helmet, gloves

The term 'klettersteig' is a bit of an exaggeration for this route, as there is only a small handful of very short sections of cable. In reality it is a fun, adventurous hike with a few sections of scrambling and assisted climbing. The views down to Innsbruck and across to the far peaks are superb, and reaching a great summit and a mountain hut is an added bonus to finish with. Due to the easy nature of the route, it is also suitable for physically capable or slightly older children.

As you get off the lift, there is a small path signposted 'Glungezer Klettersteig' that you should follow briefly to arrive onto a wide green path, which serves as a ski piste in the winter. Follow the piste, which runs parallel to a drag lift (out of use in summer), until the small station at the top of the drag lift. From here a small path branches off right from the piste, again signposted 'Glungezer Klettersteig'. Follow this path uphill for around 10mins, and just after it passes under a two-man

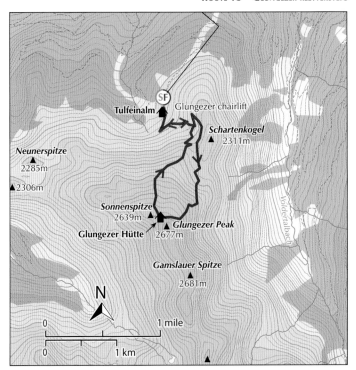

chairlift, you will see some red and white markings on the rock ahead and right, pointing you towards the start of the klettersteig. Note – this could be quite easy to miss! Follow these markings through a boulder field, initially along a vague path, until you end up on a short and easy ridge scramble.

Continue following the markers, dropping off to the right and doubling back slightly across a boulder scree field, where another short ridge leads to the foot of the klettersteig. Allow 50mins walking from the top of the lift. From here the route is clearer: there are three short stretches of cable, often narrow and quite adventurous, which are intersperced with sections of hiking or scrambling, and soon the Glungezer Hütte will come into view. A final climb along the hiking path will bring you out at the **Glungezer Hütte**. Optional extras from the hut are to take further paths which lead to the two summits of the Glungezer and the Sonnenspitze.

Perched proudly between the Glungezer Peak and the Sonnenspitze, Glungezer Hütte (tel 05223 78018, **www.glungezer.at**, open June until October and December until April) has unrivalled panoramic views and has even won a number of awards for its cuisine. It is said that on a clear day more than 500 summits can be seen from the hut.

To descend, follow the marked hiking trail downhill, parallel with the ascent route, bearing left back down to **Glungezer chairlift** to descend to Tulfes.

One of the few sections of cable on the Glungezer klettersteig

ROUTE 14

Brandjochspitze

Start/Finish	Mid-station (Seegrube) of the Hungerburg lift
Ascent	690m (290m climbing on the ridge)
Grade	3
Time	6hrs 30mins (2hr 30min walk-in, 2hrs climbing, 2hr walk-down)
Terrain	Hiking trails and rocky ridge climbing
High point	2559m
Maps	Kompass Map 36 Innsbruck Brenner or Map 036 Innsbruck und Umgebung
Public transport	Public bus from Innsbruck centre to the Hungerburg cable car station or from Innsbruck centre, take the funicular railway up to the Hungerburg station.
Access and parking	It is possible to drive up to Hungerburg and park there.
Equipment	30m rope, five quickdraws, small selection of nuts, cams and slings, belay device

This is a fantastic scramble along the southern ridge of the Brandjochspitze, in a wonderful location high above Innsbruck. With a couple of sections of grade 3 this is a challenging scramble where you might be glad of a rope occasionally. The views across the Inn Valley from the ridge are spectacular and the 360-degree panorama from the summit is well worth the effort of getting there.

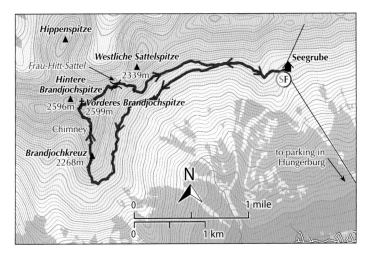

From the Seegrube cable car station, follow the path traversing west signposted 'Vorderes Brandjoch'. There are a multitude of paths branching off, but ensure you stay low, despite this often feeling counterintuitive. High above you to the right you will see the cross which marks the summit of Brandjochkreuz. Continue traversing the hillside. It will feel like you have gone too far, but you haven't, keep going until you reach a large flat area with no trees or bushes. From here make the gruelling 30min climb up a steep path to the summit cross of **Brandjochkreuz**. This marks the start of the ridge climb.

The route begins with some easy scrambling either along or just off the ridge itself, following the occasional cairn and rather hard to spot yellow paint mark. At 2400m altitude you will reach a 25m-high **chimney** marked with a yellow arrow where you may feel happier roped up if not already. There is a large metal stake 5m up the chimney so you know you are still on route.

Do not look down!

At the top of the chimney you will emerge onto a very exposed section of ridge crest, culminating in a tricky and exposed step down across a gap. From here follow a further section of exposed ridge ground to work your way back onto the crest of the ridge, downclimb to a small notch and follow the easy grassy ground round to the left and into a large scree-filled gully. Follow a vague path up this gully and onto the final summit ridge where an easy scramble will bring you to the summit cross at the top of **Brandjochspitze**.

To descend, follow a well-marked path down the scree slope which forms the east ridge of Brandjochspitze. The path is occasionally exposed and there are short sections of via ferrata cable, but the terrain is easy and leads to the **Frau-Hitt-Sattel** (col). From here clear signposts will bring you back to **Seegrube**.

ROUTE 15

Nordgrat–Vordere Sommerwand

Start/Finish	Oberissalm
Ascent	900m (430m climbing on the ridge)
Grade	3
Time	7hrs (1hr 15min walk-in, 45mins to the foot of the route, 2hrs 30mins climbing, 2hrs 30mins walk-down)
Terrain	Hiking trails and rocky ridge climbing
High point	2676m
Maps	Kompass Map 83 Stubaier Alpen or Map 36 Innsbruck Brenner
Public transport	None (Oberissalm is very difficult to reach without a car).
Access and parking	From the centre of Milders, turn right directly after the Intersport shop and before the Farm Bar, signposted 'Oberbergtal'. Follow the narrow single-track road for 10km to arrive at Oberissalm where there is paid parking.
Equipment	Harness, 50m rope, six quickdraws, belay device

Towering impressively above the Franz-Senn Hütte in the Stubaital, the north ridge of the Vordere Sommerwand is a fantastic ridge climb. The route follows the ridge right up to the summit cross, and provides 430m of easy and very enjoyable scrambling. The whole route is bolted, and with a maximum difficulty of grade 3 in a few sections you may be glad of a rope, but in general the terrain is a fun scramble. The Franz-Senn Hütte is a popular spot for hikers, however, you are unlikely to see many fellow climbers on the route making it all the more enjoyable.

Oberissalm is currently being leased and not open to the public.

From Oberissalm there is a clear, well-signposted path for the Franz-Senn Hütte. Follow this very pleasant hiking path for approximately 1hr 15mins to reach the **Franz-Senn Hütte**.

*Franz-Senn Hütte (tel 05226 2218, **www.franzsennhuette.at**, open mid June until mid October) is a well-known and very popular mountain hut with hikers and mountaineers. Originally built in 1885, it is modern and comfortable while still retaining all its original charm. It even offers wireless internet.*

From the hut, the ridge can be clearly seen rising up behind it. Signposted 'Vordere Sommerwand', follow the winding path uphill for 45mins to reach a **boulder field** at the foot of the ridge. Just at the point where the boulders give way to the solid ridge, cross the boulder field to the foot of the ridge to find three bolts and a flat area for gearing up at the start of the climb. There is a very vague path leading up to this but it may not be visible.

From here follow the ridge line up, following either bolts, bits of tat or cairns nearer the top. There are a couple of tricky moves near the beginning, and the crux is a slab around halfway up the route. However, the slab is short and well

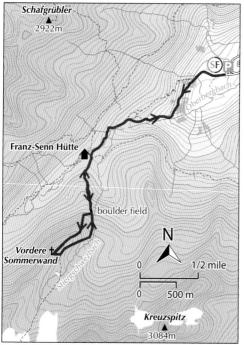

bolted. Follow the bolts with a rope and it should not be too difficult. If in doubt simply follow the easiest and most worn line up the crest of the ridge. Some parts of the route are quite exposed but with bolted belays it is possible to pitch sections at any point.

Where the angle of the ridge flattens out onto a grassy section, you will be able to see the summit cross above you. The final section is slightly exposed yet easy scrambling to reach the **summit**, from where you will be rewarded with a stunning 360-degree panorama.

You will almost certainly have this ridge to yourselves

Begin the descent by walking down the same way you came up, and after 5mins you will reach the small grassy area; the last section of grass before the ridge becomes entirely boulders. Here there is an easy-to-miss descent path on your right as you are descending, signalled with a red paint marker. This path winds its way back down to the Franz-Senn Hütte, and from here retrace your steps back down to **Oberissalm**.

ROUTE 16
Nordgrat Zwölferkogel

Start/Finish	Alpenrose Hotel, Kühtai
Ascent	970m (380m climbing on the ridge)
Grade	3 (mostly grade 1 and 2)
Time	6hrs (1hr 30min walk-in, 2hrs 30mins climbing, 2hr walk-down)
Terrain	Hiking trails and rocky ridge climbing
High point	2988m
Maps	Kompass Map 35 Imst – Telfs – Kühtai – Mieminger Kette or Map 290 Rund um Innsbruck
Public transport	There is a direct bus to Kühtai from Innsbruck.
Access and parking	Pass straight through the village of Kühtai and drop down the other side to soon see the distinctive pink building of the Alpenrose Hotel on the left behind the Dreiseenbahn chairlift. Park here to begin the walk-in.
Equipment	Harness, 30m rope, six quickdraws, small selection of wires, cams and slings

If you have spent any time in the ski area of Kühtai you will most certainly have spotted the very distinctive Zwölferkogel peak rising high above the valley and overlooking the equally impressive and photogenic reservoir. The north ridge of the Zwölferkogel is a spectacular 380m scramble with a maximum grade of 3. The walk-in may feel like a bit of a slog at times and there are a couple of exposed sections on the route where most will be glad of a rope, but this excellent scramble is absolutely worth the effort to reach a peak just shy of 3000m.

Alpenrose Hotel (tel 05239 5205, **www.hotel-alpenrose.eu**, open in winter only)

From the Alpenrose Hotel begin walking up the paved road under the cables of the chairlift, initially in the direction of the dam wall. Follow this road for around 40mins to reach the **Graf-Ferdinand-Haus** alpine hut.

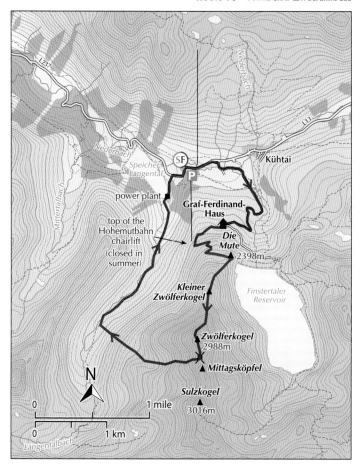

Graf-Ferdinand-Haus Hut (tel 05239 21666, **www.graf-ferdinand.at**, only open during the winter)

Take the steep path behind the hut and climb for around 20mins to arrive at the top of the **Hohemutbahn chairlift** (not in use in the summer). Some 30 metres before reaching the lift station a vague path branches off to the left. Follow

91

Starting the descent

this uphill for 10mins to a col, from where there is no real path but head up the grassy, rocky north-facing ridge above which eventually leads to the top of the **Kleiner Zwölferkogel**, where the climbing begins.

Start out along the ridge, which is generally easy scrambling but can occasionally be exposed in parts, onto a subsidiary summit, from where the rest of the route reveals itself above. The remainder of the scramble features several steeper and trickier towers which, although never very difficult climbing, can be rather exposed, and all but the most confident scramblers will be glad of a rope in parts.

There are no fixed bolts in place and very little to help you route find, however, with the reservoir below on your left, you need to simply follow the crest of the ridge, occasionally dropping off to either side where the terrain is steeper or trickier.

From the summit of **Zwölferkogel**, scramble down the rocky path southwards onto the wide saddle between the Zwölferkogel and the Mittagsköpfl. From the **saddle** turn right to start descending a rocky scree slope and follow this for around 1hr 30mins, all the way down to the valley floor, until you reach the river. Turn right following the river, passing a **power plant** after 2km, to reach a road, where you turn right and a further 10mins uphill will bring you back to the **Alpenrose Hotel**.

The Bettelwurfhütte (Route 17)

A mountain hut is often a great goal for a walk and can also provide a logical halfway point for a longer, multi-day hike. In the mountains around Innsbruck alone there are in excess of 70 huts, many of which also have accommodation and are often buried deep in the heart of the mountains, providing a secluded and blissful spot for an overnight stay.

Mountain huts are generally busy during the day, with hikers and mountain bikers stopping to recharge, however, the evenings and the early mornings are quiet and peaceful, a perfect time to experience the mountains at their best. The added benefit of staying in a hut, as opposed to camping, is of course that you need to carry little more than what you would take on a day hike. The huts provide bedding, dinner, breakfast and occasionally a packed lunch for an extra cost. It is always advisable to check whether the hut is open before you leave, as there is always the potential that they have not updated their website, or that it is closed for refurbishment or damage. It is also essential to make a reservation beforehand to avoid disappointment upon arrival.

It proved very difficult to whittle the multi-day, overnight possibilities around Innsbruck down to just a

Beautiful scenery at the top of the Rofan gondola (Route 20)

few. Described here are just a small selection of great two- or three-day trips, staying in some of Tirol's finest huts and taking in some spectacular scenery. The terrain is varied, passing mountain lakes, forest trails, spectacular rock walls and alpine meadows, and one of the hikes can even be tackled as either a walk or a via ferrata, opening up further options.

ROUTE 17
Halltal hike

Start/Finish	Absam
Distance	18km, or 11.2km following the return route option
Ascent	1510m
Time	2 days (day 1 – 4hrs; day 2 – 3hrs 30mins)
Terrain	Well established walking path with short sections of easy scrambling
High point	2223m
Maps	Kompass Map 26 Karwendelgebirge
Public transport	A direct bus will take you from Innsbruck to Absam.
Access and parking	From Hall in Tirol, take the Salzbergstraße following signs for Absam Gnadenwald. After 3km at the four-way junction continue straight on to Halltal and you will shortly reach the large car park in front of the entrance to the Hall Valley; indicated by a large banner sign welcoming you to the Karwendel: 'Herzlich Willkommen Alpenpark Karwendel'. This is the end of the vehicle access and from here you can only enter the Karwendel on foot.
Huts	Bettelwurfhütte

The beautiful, secluded and seldom-visited Halltal Valley is one of Tirol's secrets. This two-day hike provides a very satisifying round trip (although you can return the way you ascended if preferred, taking 2½ hours). Day 1 of the route, from Absam up to the Bettelwurfhütte, can be tackled either as a hiking trail for those who prefer to stay on firm ground or alternatively as a thoroughly enjoyable via ferrata. The hiking route is described below; for the via ferrata, see Route 38 (Absamer klettersteig).

Day 1 – Absam to Bettelwurfhütte
5.6km, 1270m ascent, 4hrs
From the carpark in Absam, follow the tarmac road north-northwest into the Halltal Valley itself for 20mins until you reach a series of concrete buildings on

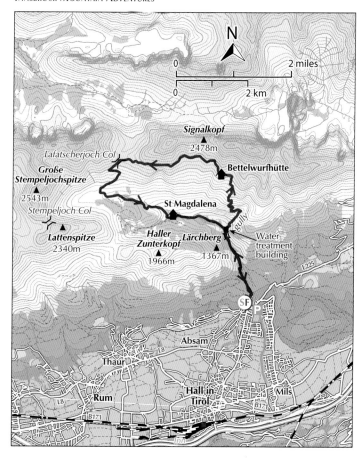

the right and a **bridge** crossing the river. (There is a sign here telling you to carry on straight up the road if you want to do the Absamer klettersteig or to turn right if you want to 'just' walk up the hut.) Go over the bridge and follow red and white paint marks which denote the path.

Follow the path uphill for 15–20mins to a path split. Go right and continue to climb (by now quite steeply) towards a huge scree-filled gully. When the path reaches the **gully** it climbs up some steep, loose and frankly unpleasant scree on

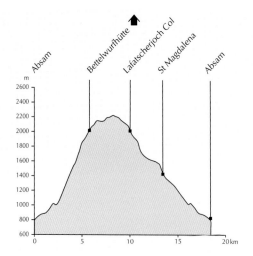

the right-hand side of the gully and then traverses across the gully to the far side. There is then an exposed 100-metre traverse which is protected by a handrail cable. The terrain underfoot is easy but a head for heights is required. Once at the end of the cables, the path once again becomes a normal walking trail.

Follow the path for 30mins, at which point the Bettelwurfhütte will emerge into view above and left of you. Continue up for a further hour to reach it on a steep path with the occasional section of very easy slabby scrambling en route.

> Built at the end of the 19th century, Bettelwurfhütte (tel 05223 53353, **www.bettelwurfhuette.at**, 32 bunk beds, 30 mattresses on the floor, open early June to mid October) offers incredible views across Hall in Tirol and Innsbruck and is popular with both hikers and ski tourers.

Day 2 – Bettelwurfhütte to Absam
12.4km, 240m ascent, 3hrs 30mins
From the hut, follow the clear path west for 1hr 30mins on an undulating and rocky path to the **Lafatscherjoch Col** (2081m). There are several sections where the path crosses riverbeds and scree bowls and these will be threatened by rock-fall in early summer (when there is still snow melting above them) or when it is raining hard and causing rocks to move. Choose your spots for a rest carefully and, if in doubt, keep moving. There are also very short sections of cable and

An unexpected friend en route

metal staples to get you across some of the rockier sections. The col is broad, grassy and enjoys wonderful views, making for an ideal spot for a break.

Continue west towards the **Stempeljoch Col** for 10mins to reach a path branching off left, signposted for St Magdalena. Take this path and descend passing **St Magdalena** to the foot of the valley and follow the tarmac road for 1hr 30mins back to **Absam**.

ROUTE 18

Nordkette traverse

Start	Top station (Hafelekar) of the Hungerburg lift
Finish	Absam
Distance	19.7km
Ascent/Descent	770m/2050m
Time	3 days (day 1 – 2hrs; day 2 – 4hrs 30mins; day 3 – 2hrs 30mins)
Terrain	Well-maintained rocky mountain paths
High point	2288m
Maps	Kompass Map 36 Innsbruck Brenner or Map 036 Innsbruck und Umgebung
Public transport	Public bus from Innsbruck centre to the Hungerburg cable car station or the funicular railway. At the end, a regular and direct bus runs between Absam and Innsbruck. See below for cable car details.
Access and parking	It is possible to drive directly up to Hungerburg and park at the lift station in the pay and display car park, however, as the hike starts and finishes in different places this is not ideal. From Hungerburg, take the cable car up to Seegrube, and then change to continue up to the higher station of Hafelekar.
Huts	Pfeishütte and Bettelwurfhütte

The ridge following the Nordkette chain dominates the skyline to the north of Innsbruck. To the south the views across the Inn Valley to the Patscherkofel summit and the Brenner Pass are simply breathtaking and, to the north, the wild feeling of the virtually empty Karwendel is a sight rarely found in the European Alps today. Although the walking days are relatively short, covering between 5km and 9km per day, this is a classic multi-day walking route and will not fail to impress. Hikers will take in two of Tirol's wildest and most well-known huts, and for each day there are several optional variants for those who wish to extend the journey and add some extra peaks. With a lift to access the starting point, an undulating, thoroughly enjoyable path throughout, several extra hikes and peaks to tag along the way and two fantastic alpine huts to feed and accommodate you, you will not be disappointed by this three-day hike. The path, marked with red and white paint markers for the majority of the route, is very easy to follow.

Day 1 – Hafelekar to Pfeishütte
5.2km, 220m ascent, 2hrs

Exit the **Hafelekar lift station** and, although not signposted, take the narrow path to the Pfeishütte which leads directly down and to the right, traversing around the hillside to the east.

Variant

A nice variation which adds on an extra 10mins is to follow the zigzagging path up to the small peak above the station. Marked with a large cross, this is a great view point across Innsbruck. From here traverse around the back of the peak to quickly rejoin the path which leads from the cable car.

Shortly after the two paths converge you will pass a series of yellow signs; stay on the main rocky path, following the direction of the Goetheweg, which hugs the

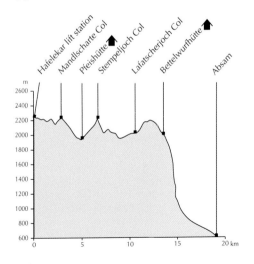

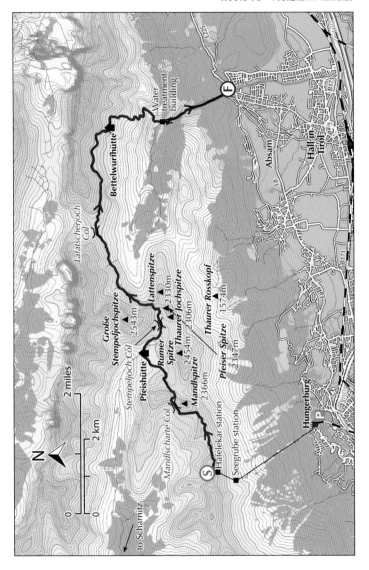

One of the empty valleys of the Karwendel

rock face and provides fantastic views across the Inn Valley. The path starts on the south side of the ridge, then briefly nips over to the north side, with a completely different vista across the Karwendel.

About 20mins into the hike you will reach a yellow sign telling you that the Pfeishütte is 1hr 45 mins away. After a short, steep uphill section and a further 20mins on you will reach the north side of the ridge and soon afterwards head downhill. A split in the path gives you the option of a short detour up to the right to tag on an excellent little summit – the **Mandlspitze** (2366m) – otherwise, bear left to continue along the main path to the Pfeishütte. A mainly downhill, varied and constantly picturesque route leads along the north side of the ridge, and after a steep but short final uphill climb up to a small notch, you will reach the **Mandlscharte Col** (2277m) with a yellow sign indicating Pfeishütte is 40mins away. From here head down the rocky and winding path, keeping left at each junction to follow the hut signs, to shortly reach **Pfeishütte** itself (1922m).

Pfeishütte (tel 0720 316596, **www.pfeishuette.at**, 30 bunk beds, 50 mattresses on the floor, open mid June to mid October) is a very quaint hut, nestled in a valley basin and surrounded on all sides by impressive mountains. It is well known for its fine cuisine and friendly resident dog.

Day 1 extensions
To make day 1 into a longer day it is also possible to begin this route from Scharnitz, an easy train ride or a 40min drive from Innsbruck, rather than starting

from Hafelekar. The Pfeishütte alpine hut is a 5hr walk from Scharnitz through a beautiful, quiet valley, therefore providing an alternative starting point.

Another great, albeit more adventurous, extension to day 1 would be to combine it with the first section of the Innsbrucker klettersteig (Route 31) which also starts from the **Hafelekar station**. The via ferrata takes around 4hrs and finishes at the Seegrube lift station, from where you could take the cable car back up to Hafelekar to start the day 1 hike to Pfeishütte.

Day 2 – Pfeishütte to Bettelwurfhütte
9km, 550m ascent, 4hrs 30mins
From Pfeishütte, a sign directly outside the hut points left for the Bettelwurfhütte. Keep right at the junction soon afterwards to head uphill and follow the well-marked trail for 1–1hr 30mins to the **Stempeljoch Col** (2215m).

Detours
There are numerous extra peaks which can be 'bagged' easily from here, including the **Pfeiser Spitze** (2347m) and the **Thaurer Jochspitze** (2306m), both of which are well worth detouring to and are only 30mins from the col. For those keener for an even bigger detour, the **Lattenspitze** (2330m) is an hour from the col.

The Pfeishütte

From the Stempeljoch, descend the steep scree slope to the east for 150 metres. The path leads leftwards and deposits you under the rocky east face of the Stempeljochspitze peak (2529m).

From here, follow the clear but rocky (and sometimes exposed) path for 1hr 30mins as it undulates to the **Lafatscherjoch Col** (2081m). The path is continually rocky underfoot and this makes it quite tiring but reaching the Lafatscherjoch is a great reward – the col is wide, grassy and offers expansive 360-degree views.

From the col, continue for another 1hr 30mins on a similar undulating and rocky path to the Bettelwurfhütte (2077m). There are several sections where the path crosses riverbeds and scree bowls and these will be threatened by rockfall in early summer; choose your spots for a rest carefully and if in doubt keep moving. There are also very short sections of cable and metal staples to get you across some of the rockier sections. **Bettelwurfhütte** is visible for much of the final half hour and it looks stunning, perched high above the Halltal Valley.

> Built at the end of the 19th century, Bettelwurfhütte (tel 05223 53353, **www.bettelwurfhuette.at**, 32 bunk beds, 30 mattresses on the floor, open early June to mid October) offers incredible views across Hall in Tirol and Innsbruck and is popular with both hikers and ski tourers.

Day 3 – Bettelwurfhütte to Absam
5.6km, 1445m descent, 2hrs 30mins
From the front terrace of the Bettelwurfhütte, follow the clear path due east which winds downwards for 2hrs to emerge onto the approach road next to a **water treatment building**. From here follow the road back down to the car park in **Absam**.

ROUTE 19

Karwendel traverse

Start	Scharnitz
Finish	Stans
Distance	51km
Ascent/Descent	2300m/2700m
Time	3 days (day 1 – 5hrs; day 2 – 8hrs; day 3 – 4hrs 30mins)
Terrain	Well-maintained hiking paths
High point	1953m
Maps	Kompass Map 26 Karwendelgebirge
Public transport	Scharnitz can be easily reached via a direct train from Innsbruck, and there is a direct train back from Stans to Innsbruck, an ideal option.
Access and parking	Having passed through Scharnitz, take a right-hand road directly after the large cream-coloured church on the right-hand side of the road, signposted to Karwendeltaler, and pass a grassy parking area on your left where the road splits. Take the right-hand fork following Hinterautalstrasse and after 50 metres you will cross a bridge and reach the parking area on the right-hand side with a pay and display machine and a large wooden signpost on the left showing a number of walking routes and timings. If this area is full you can also use the large grassy area 100 metres back down the road.
Huts	Karwendelhaus and Lamsenjochhütte

This superb three-day hike is one of the classic Tirol routes, covering a fantastic section of the Karwendel mountain range, and taking in several sections of the famous 'Eagle Walk' which traverses Tirol. Due to its relative remoteness, the entire route is exceptionally quiet, and the solitude alone is well worth the effort. As well as the two overnight destinations, you will pass a number of fantastic mountain huts. All are welcoming, friendly and excellent value for money, so there is no danger of going hungry en route! The views throughout are second to none, and you can be safe in the knowledge that you are among a precious few who make the effort to tackle this route and have the opportunity to witness nature at its best.

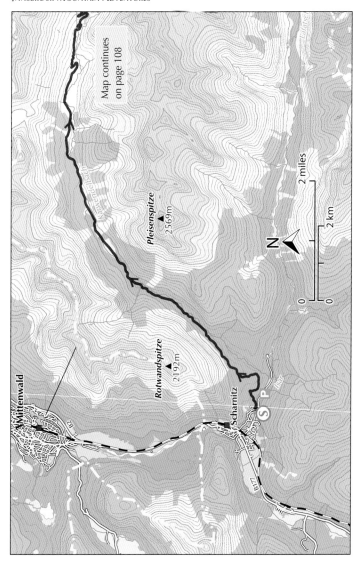

Map continues on page 108

Pleisenspitze
▲ 2569m

Rotwandspitze
▲ 2192m

Mittenwald

Scharnitz

S P

N

2 miles

2 km

0

0

Day 1 – Scharnitz to Karwendelhaus
18km, 800m ascent, 5hrs

The Karwendeltal and Karwendelhaus are marked on the large wooden signpost next to the parking area. Follow the track as directed and 50 metres later the road branches off right, again signposted for Karwendeltal and Karwendelhaus, and from there you simply follow a well-established 4x4 track, ignoring any subsidiary roads, all the way to the Karwendelhaus, your bed for the night. The first 4hrs is a thoroughly enjoyable, gentle track, mostly flat with a few undulations, with the final hour being a bit of an uphill grind making **Karwendelhaus** a welcome sight.

> Over 100 years old, the Karwendelhaus (tel 0720 983554, **www. karwendelhaus.com**, 52 bunk beds, 141 mattresses on the floor, open early June to mid October), overlooking a secluded valley, is an impressive hut deservedly popular with day trippers either hiking or mountain biking. It boasts a truly stunning location, with an old-fashioned wooden interior and hearty, inexpensive food.

Day 2 – Karwendelhaus to Lamsenjochhütte
20.5km, 1305m ascent, 8hrs

From the Karwendelhaus, follow a short climb to **Hochalmsattel** and then continue downhill on the 4x4 track. Shortly after the descent begins, take the walking

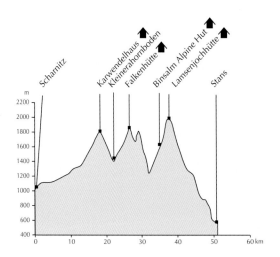

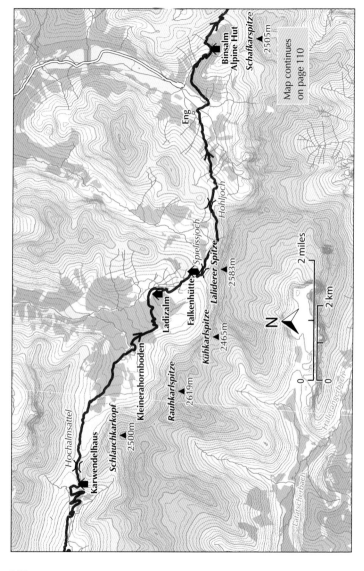

Binsalm Alpine Hut

Schafkarspitze

2505m

Map continues on page 110

Eng

Hohljoch

Spielissjoch

Laliderer Spitze

2583m

Falkenhütte

Ladizalm

Kühkarlspitze

2465m

Rauhkarlspitze

2619m

Kleinerahornboden

Schlauchkarkopf

2500m

Hochalmsattel

Karwendelhaus

N

2 miles

2 km

0

0

Lafatscherbach

Hallerangerbach

The impressively located Karwendelhaus

trail which branches off left, winding down through alpine pastures and leaving the wider track for mountain bikers. After 5km of downhill walking this trail will eventually bring you out at **Kleinerahornboden**, a four-way junction with two lovely wooden chalets. If you missed the walking trail and stayed on the 4x4 track you still emerge at Kleinerahornboden, albeit having walked marginally further.

From Kleinerahordboden continue straight ahead, following signs for Hinteriss and Falkenhütte. Some 50 metres after the junction at Kleinerahornboden, take the hiking trail which branches off right at a small bridge. The trail traverses around the hillside and then ascends to a junction with a wider track. Continue ascending, now on the 4x4 track, following signs for Falkenhütte. After 15mins you will pass **Ladizalm**, a small collection of chalets, and from here it is just a 30min climb up to **Falkenhütte**.

From the hut, take the 4x4 track down to **Spielissjoch saddle**, where the route becomes narrower and eventually reaches **Hohljoch Col** and then winds gently down through alpine fields to the hamlet of **Eng**. From Eng follow a dirt road that climbs upwards and continue until you reach **Binsalm Alpine Hut**. The route then continues up to **Western Lamsenjoch Saddle** before finally heading down to the **Lamsenjochhütte** (1953m).

Lamsenjochhütte (tel 05244 62063, **www.lamsenjochhuette.at**, 22 bunk beds, 94 mattresses on the floor, open June until mid October) is very popular

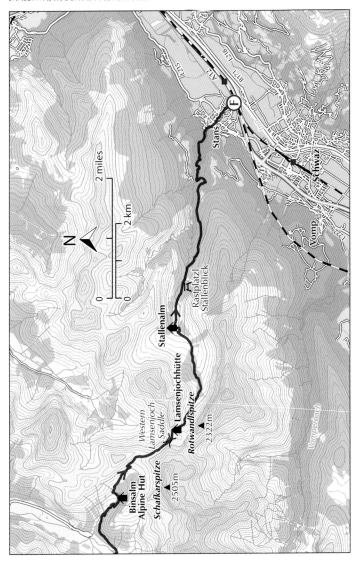

as a base for hikers and climbers. It was built in 1906 and was destroyed in an avalanche just two years later.

Day 3 – Lamsenjochhütte to Stans
12.5km, 1390m descent, 4hrs 30mins

From the Lamsenjochhütte walk briefly downhill before taking the right fork onto a trail which heads out of the valley. Eventually the trail rejoins the road, which will take you downhill through the forest. Continue downhill until you leave the road, following signs for 'Stallenalm'. Here you must cross the stream; if this proves difficult you can continue onwards along the road as the routes merge further ahead.

Wildflowers high above the valley

Continue past Stallenalm and take the flat path before crossing the riverbed to find yourself at the **Rastplatzl Stallenblick picnic area**. Head back into the forest and take the path leading downhill, passing another picnic area. Follow the signs for Fiecht and Vomp, leading gently downhill before taking the footpath on the left towards St Georgen, Wolfsklamm and Stans. Continue down through the forest until the trail meets another 4x4 track. From here turn left to continue downhill, and at the junction head towards Wolfsklamm on the left-hand side of the river. The next section of the path criss-crosses the river, aided by a fixed line of cables. Soon after leaving the river you will reach a dirt road, follow this to arrive in the village of **Stans**. After the church you will find the Stans train station, with direct trains back to Innsbruck, or changing in Innsbruck for a train back to Scharnitz.

ROUTE 20
Rofan Range hike

Start	Kramsach
Finish	Erfurter Hütte, or Maurach
Distance	19km
Ascent	2050m
Time	2 days (day 1 – 6hrs; day 2 – 3hrs 30mins, or 5hrs if not using the lift)
Terrain	Well-established hiking paths
High point	2002m
Maps	Kompass Map 027 Achensee
Public transport	Due to having different start and finish points the logistics of this route are not straightforward, however, it is possible both by car and public transport. A bus will take you from Innsbruck to Kramsach, changing once in Brixlegg, taking just over an hour. Make sure you get off at stop 'Kramsach Sonnwendjochbahn'. To return from Maurach take a bus changing in Jenbach to Innsbruck (or take the train from Jenbach to Innsbruck), again in just over an hour. The other option is to leave your car in either Maurach, and take the public bus to the start of the hike in Kramsach, or, alternatively, leave the car in Kramsach, then take the bus back from Maurach to Kramsach, changing in Jenbach and Brixlegg and taking just over an hour.
Access and parking	From Innsbruck follow the A12 east for 44km to take exit 32 towards Kramsach and Brixlegg. Keep right to cross back over the motorway then at the roundabout take the first exit then the immediate left onto Ländbühel. Follow this for 700 metres, then take the left-hand turning onto Wittberg, signposted 'Bergbahn Sonnwendjoch', and continue for 500 metres to see the chairlift parking on the left (lift no longer in use).
Huts	Bayreuther Hütte
Note	It is advised to book accommodation in the Bayreuther Hütte in advance to avoid disappointment, especially in high season.

The Rofan mountain range high above Achensee Lake is a particularly beautiful part of Tirol. Unspoilt and one of the quieter parts of the region, this area is known for its rugged beauty, outstanding wilderness and emerald-coloured mountain lakes. This incredibly scenic two-day trek is challenging in parts, yet you will be fully rewarded for your efforts throughout. The spectacular scenery along the way is of course worth the effort alone, but the addition of excellent mountain huts and a visit to Zireiner See Lake, widely considered to be one of the most beautiful in Tirol, is a real added bonus. Hikers could previously cut out the initial and most strenuous part of the hike by taking the Sonnwendjochbahn chairlift up to the Berghaus Sonnwendjoch hut, however unfortunately this lift is no longer in operation.

Day 1 – Kramsach to Bayreuther Hütte
11km, 1400m ascent, 6hrs

From the car park at the bottom of the Sonnwendjochbahn chairlift, you will see a series of yellow signs pointing uphill along a gravel track behind the lift station. Follow path number 9, direction Bayreuther Hütte and Sonnwendjoch, and follow it until it divides, then take the right-hand path signposted for Kaltwasserbründl. Continue as far as the mid-station of the chairlift, and from there follow the steep

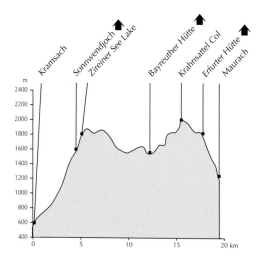

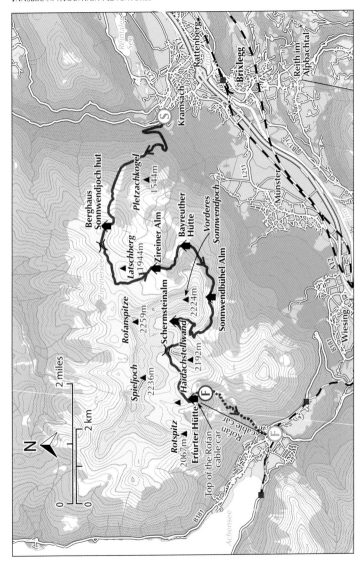

trail 8a which follows the route the lift used to take, using the overhead cables as a guide to keep you on track. Around 3hrs 30mins after leaving the car park you will emerge at the top of the lift and the very welcoming **Sonnwendjoch hut** (1770m), an ideal place for a break after the fairly challenging start! While here, make sure you do not miss getting a birds-eye view of the landscape through the special telescope viewer which is installed at the top station of the Sonnwendjochbahn. There are six of these sightseeing telescopes installed throughout the 'Eagle Walk', Tirol's most famous long-distance hiking trail.

From the hut, continue upwards onto the **Rosskogelsattel**, passing under the Rosskogel peak, until you reach marked trail 411. Turn left, following this pleasant path downhill until you reach the **Zireinersee Lake**, allowing 1hr from the hut to the lake. From the western end of the lake, follow a short stretch uphill to reach a split in the path. Take the left fork along trail 412, signposted for Zireiner Alm and Bayreuther Hütte (1600m). A further 1hr 30mins will bring you to the **Bayreuther Hütte**, your accommodation for the night and no doubt a welcome sight.

Quiet and sunny, Bayreuther Hütte (tel 0664 3425103, **www. bayreuther-huette.de**, 24 bunk beds, 28 mattresses on the floor, open from May/June until mid October) is set in a beautiful location.

Day 2 – Bayreuther Hütte to Maurach
8km, 650m ascent, 3hrs 30mins (5hrs if not using the lift)
From the Bayreuther Hütte, take hiking trail 22 which undulates west, skirting around the Vorderes Sonnwendjoch to the right, and passing **Sonnwendbühel**

Stunning Lake Achensee, a just reward at the end of your hike

Why not top off your hike with an exhilarating ride on the flying fox at the end?

Alm. At the split, head north on trail 21 for a steep but short climb up to the **Schermstein Alm** (1855m). From here take path number 16 heading westwards to follow an occasionally steep yet enjoyable trail around Haidachstellwand to reach the **Krahnsattel Col**, the route's high point at 2002m. Enjoy the uninterrupted views from this col, which include the Rosskopf Peak, the Seekarlspitze and the Rotspitze.

From here path 15B starts to slowly descend towards the **Erfurter Hütte** at the top of the Rofan cable car and the end of the hike. The area at the top of the cable car is a very popular area for both hiking and rock climbing.

The lift will take you down to **Maurach** or, alternatively for those who feel they have not quite had enough of hiking, the descent path takes around 1hr 30mins.

⊗ ALPINE MOUNTAINEERING

Looking across the Stubai peaks from the Wilder Freiger summit ridge (Route 22)

Austria may not be the first place that springs to mind when considering tackling some alpine mountaineering routes, but despite its lack of hallowed 4000m peaks, Austria packs a great punch when it comes to enjoyable, mid-grade mountaineering. And as most of Austria's peaks are lesser known than their French or Swiss counterparts, rather than standing in line at bottlenecks and having to share the summit with a crowd of other climbers, you will instead experience less crowded routes which are therefore often much safer and more enjoyable. Austria is known as the hidden gem of the Alps, and this rings particularly true with regards to alpine mountaineering.

However, mountaineering in Austria should by no means be taken lightly. The vast majority of the high alpine routes are glaciated and well over 3000m. Walking on glaciers and moving at high altitude is dangerous and it is important not to understate the risks of undertaking such an activity without the required knowledge, experience and expertise. The correct equipment must be carried at all times and hiring a mountain guide is highly recommended for those lacking the

117

Arriving at the Mitterkarjoch Col (Route 24)

necessary mountain experience. Most alpine routes are well travelled and often no more than a snow-plod, but when moving on glaciated terrain it is important to understand correct techniques such as basic rope skills, how to walk or climb roped together, and emergency rescue should your partner fall into a crevasse. The routes included here centre on the well-known peaks in the Ötztal Alps and the Stubai Alps, the main mountaineering areas near Innsbruck.

The alpine mountaineering routes in this guide are graded in accordance with the standard mountaineering grades, ranging from F (facile – easy), through PD (peu difficile – a little difficult) to AD (assez difficile – quite difficult) and above. PD+ is the most difficult route included in this guide. Timings are given in terms of how many days are needed, and rough walking times. All of the routes in this section involve an overnight stay at an alpine hut, the route to which is described in the 'Approach' section.

The minimum equipment required for an alpine route is a 35m rope plus slings and karabiners for each person. For glaciated terrain you may also need crampons and an ice axe, however, the routes described each have a detailed list of what you will need for each individual ascent.

ROUTE 21
Habicht

Start	Neustift, top of the Elferbahn or Gschnitz
Finish	Neustift
Ascent	2310m from Neustift, 1480m from the Elferbahn cable car or 2040m from Gschnitz
Grade	PD
Time	2 days (day 1 – 4hrs 30mins, 3hrs 30mins or 3hrs, day 2 – 9hrs)
Terrain	Walking paths with short sections of via ferrata and some sections of exposed scrambling
High point	3277m
Maps	Kompass Map 35 Innsbruck Brenner
Public transport	From Innsbruck, a direct bus to Neustift takes around 50mins or to Gschnitz also around 50mins, with a change in Steinach am Brenner.
Access and parking	From the centre of Neustift take the left-hand turning onto Moos, with an easy-to-miss signpost for the Elferbahn. Park here to take the lift or to walk to Neder. To reach Gschnitz, follow the A13 from Innsbruck for 19km then take exit 19 towards Matrei/Steinach. At the junction turn right onto the B182 and follow this for 11km before turning right onto the L10 towards Gschnitz. Follow this for a further 11km to reach the village of Gschnitz.
Hut	Innsbrucker Hütte
Equipment	Harness, via ferrata lanyards, crampons (depending on the time of year)

For a long time Habicht was thought to be the highest summit in the Tirol, however, despite this not being the case, at 3277m the peak remains one of the most impressive in the Stubai range, and a fantastic tick on any mountaineer's achievement list. The view from the top is second to none, showcasing the wild beauty of not only the Stubai Alps, but also the Zillertal Alps to the east and the Dolomites to the south.

There are various options for starting points, two of which are detailed here. Logistically it is easiest to start and finish in Neustift, but if you can manage the various public transport issues, starting in Gschnitz and finishing in Neustift is a great way to climb this peak. Starting from Neustift you will ascend and descend the same way, however starting from Gschnitz provides more of an adventure by starting and finishing in different places. Whichever route you take, they converge at the Innsbrucker Hütte, where you will stay the night, and from where the final part of the ascent begins. Habicht is one of the easier 3000m peaks, with a clear path to the summit, however it has some exposed sections and is not without danger, so make sure you are well prepared and properly equipped.

Approach from Neustift
Option 1: 1400m ascent, 4hrs 30mins; option 2: 810m ascent, 3hrs 30mins
There are two options to reach the Pinnisalm (1560m) from Neustift, which is the first stop on the way to the Innsbrucker Hütte.

1   From Neustift walk along Moos for 500 metres. Cross the river, then a further 950 metres will bring you to the hamlet of **Neder** (950m). Turn right onto Pinnisweg, which soon turns into a 4x4 track which takes you all the way up past the **Issenangeralm** (1366m) to reach the Pinnisalm. This is basically a slog, albeit one in beautiful scenery, which takes 2hrs. The Pinnisalm do offer a jeep-taxi service (tel 05226 2342, www.taxi-stubai.at/pinnis-shuttle). Call first to reserve a place.

2   From the top of the **Elferbahn cable car** follow a jeep track for 500 metres south. When it doubles back to the left, continue south on a clear path and follow this as it descends, over the course of an hour, to the Pinnisalm.

From the **Pinnisalm**, follow the jeep track south-southwest for half an hour to reach the next hut – the **Karalm** (1747m). From here the Pinnisjoch Col (which is next to the Innsbrucker Hütte) is clearly visible at the head of the Pinnistal Valley. It looks an awfully long way away! In reality it is only about 2hrs away but those 2hrs are tough-going up a very wide and clear, but continually uphill, path. From the Pinnisjoch Col, the **Innsbrucker Hütte** (2370m) is immediately to the right.

Innsbrucker Hütte (tel 05276 295, **www.innsbrucker-huette.at**, 30 bunk beds, 100 mattresses on the floor, open mid June until early October) is a popular base for climbers. Built in 1884, sitting majestically below Habicht and with stunning views, the hut itself is large, well stocked and beautifully positioned.

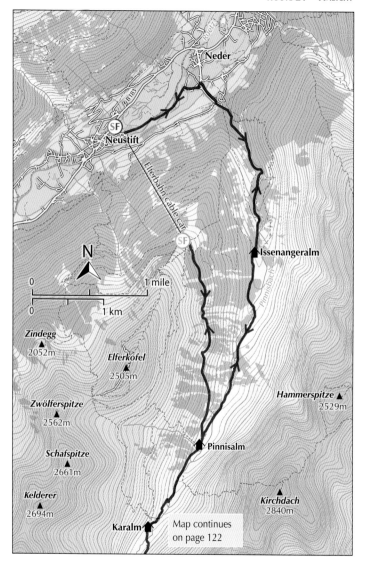

Neder

SF Neustift

Elferbahn cable car

SF

N

0   1 mile

0   1 km

Issenangeralm

Pinnisbach

Zindegg
▲ 2052m

Elferköfel
▲ 2505m

Hammerspitze ▲
2529m

Zwölferspitze ▲
2562m

Schafspitze ▲
2661m

Pinnisalm

Kelderer ▲
2694m

Kirchdach ▲
2840m

Karalm ▲

Map continues on page 122

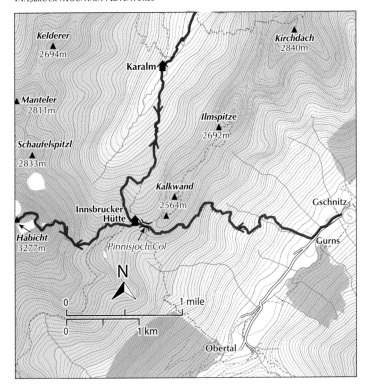

Approach from Gschnitz
1130m ascent, 3hrs

Go to the Catholic Church at the western end of **Gschnitz** (1242m) and carry on west along the road in the direction of **Gurns** for 400 metres to reach a large parking area on the right, clearly labelled as the start of the approach to the Innsbrucker Hütte.

From the parking area, follow the path as it zigzags up the hillside. There are no paths branching off and while there is minimal signposting it is hard to get lost. The path is always clear but is slightly exposed in places. It is an unrelenting climb for 3hrs and just when you are wondering if the hut will ever appear, it does, right after you come around a long right-hand bend. Once the **Innsbrucker Hütte** (2370m) is in sight it is a pleasant 10min traverse to reach it.

Alternative via Obertal

An alternative is to carry on another 2km on the road from the parking area beyond Gschnitz to reach the Gasthof Feuerstein (1281m) in the village of **Obertal** and approach the hut from here. This is more direct and tougher but there is the option of putting your rucksack on a small purpose-built cable car here and having it meet you at the hut. Whether this appeals is likely to depend on the strength of your ethics!

Ascent to the summit
905m ascent, 3hrs

The peak is clearly signposted from the hut and the sign says you will take 3hrs to reach the summit. The path is very clear for the first 10mins but after this it becomes increasingly vague. There are, however, continuous red and white paint marks to show the way as the path winds through rock and grass and climbs gradually. After 300m the path becomes increasingly steep and begins to climb a series of short rock steps which are protected by cables, and then climbs 75m of easy but exposed slabs which also have a cable running up them. Experienced scramblers with a head for heights will not need to clip in here but it is exposed and has been the scene of fatal falls. If in any doubt about your ability to scramble in an exposed position, take along a harness and some via ferrata lanyards.

The exposed slab section of the route

123

Descending the cables on the upper section of Habicht's summit ridge

Continue following the coloured paint marks, luckily, they are frequent and it is all but impossible to lose them as they guide you through a series of boulder fields and up to a large permanent snow patch to the south of Habicht's summit pyramid. In years past it was necessary to cross the snow patch but it has now shrunk and by mid summer it is possible to circumnavigate it by continuing to follow paint marks that lead you to the right of it. (As such, crampons are not usually required but may be in early summer – call the Innsbrucker Hütte before setting off to check on current conditions.) The route then curves back to the left, above the snowfield and onto the final, wide summit ridge. Follow this, staying just to the left of the crest, up more boulders and short rock steps (which are exposed but cable protected) to reach the summit of **Habicht**. Take in the incredible view of the Stubai mountains and be sure to sign the summit book.

Descent
2305m descent, 6hrs
To descend, retrace your steps back to the Innsbrucker Hütte. From the hut walk north east for 50 metres to reach the Pinnisjoch Col which is at the same altitude as the hut. From here follow the wide footpath north, clearly signposted for the Pinnisalm. The path zigzags quite steeply down to the foot of the Pinnistal Valley, to reach the Karalm. The path now becomes an easy 4x4 track. Follow it down

to the Pinnisalm, from where there are three options: take a jeep taxi down to Neustift (details in Approach, above), take the left-hand path uphill signposted for the Elferbahn cable car, or continue down the 4x4 track all the way down to the Stubai Valley and the village of Neder to finish in **Neustift**.

ROUTE 22
Wilder Freiger

Start/Finish	Grawa Alm
Ascent	1900m
Grade	F+
Time	2 days (day 1 – 2hrs, day 2 – 11hrs 30mins)
Terrain	Well-established hiking paths with sections of easy scrambling
High point	3418m
Maps	Kompass Map 36 Innsbruck Brenner, Map 036 Innsbruck und Umgebung or Map 83 Stubaier Alpen
Public transport	There is a direct bus from Innsbruck which runs regularly from Innsbruck to the Stubai ski area and stops at the Grawa Alm.
Access and parking	From Innsbruck follow the A13 for 10km then take exit 10 to Stubaier Gletscher (toll booth) and keep right at the fork to join the B183. Continue on this road for 26km and shortly after passing through Ranalt, continue on past the main parking area for the Wildewasserweg and Tschangelair Alm to reach the Grawa Waterfall itself on the left. Parking is on the right-hand side of the road, opposite the Grawa Alm and next to the huge sign for Wildewasserweg.
Hut	Sulzenauhütte (2190m)
Equipment	Crampons, ice axe

Wilder Freiger, or Cima Libera, as it is known in Italian, is one of the classic and most frequented peaks in the area. At 3418m and permanently snow covered, it is the seventh highest summit in the Stubai Alps and sits right on the border

125

between Italy and Austria. A breathtaking 360-degree view from the summit provides mountaineers with views across to the Dolomites, the Ötztal and the Hohe Tauern. There are a number of routes to the summit from both the Italian and Austrian sides. Although the walk detailed here does mean a long day of walking on the descent, it is the most accessible route when coming from the direction of Innsbruck. It is possible to break the descent by staying a second night in the Sulzenauhütte and descending back to Grawa Alm the next day.

Approach
600m ascent, 2hrs

Grawa Alm (tel 0676 4121009, www.feldhof-tirol.com, summer opening from mid May until end of September) is an understandably popular hut with easy access directly off the road, and with unrivalled views of the Grawa Waterfall.

From Grawa Alm walk around to the right-hand side to cross the river and make the short 5min journey to the waterfall itself. From here follow the wooden walkway uphill through the forest on the right-hand side of the waterfall, signposted for the Sulzenaualm and Sulzenauhütte and pass two further viewing platforms. After around 50mins you will emerge out above the trees to a beautiful view of the glacier high above. Here the path flattens out into a glacial bowl, with the **Sulzenaualm** and another fantastic waterfall up ahead.

The Sulzenaualm (tel 0676 5603090, www.sulzenau-alm.at, open from May until October) provides rather idyllic views and a perfect place to stop for a break before continuing upwards.

High up ahead you can now see the next stop on the route, the Sulzenauhütte, teetering seemingly precariously on the plateau at the top of the waterfall. From the alm, cross the glacial bowl towards the waterfall to reach a sign indicating that the Sulzenauhütte can be reached by following either direction. Both paths merge later on and lead to the hut so it does not matter which one you choose. Follow the path winding upwards for another 45mins to reach **Sulzenauhütte** and enjoy the breathtaking views both up towards the glacier and back down across the glacial basin.

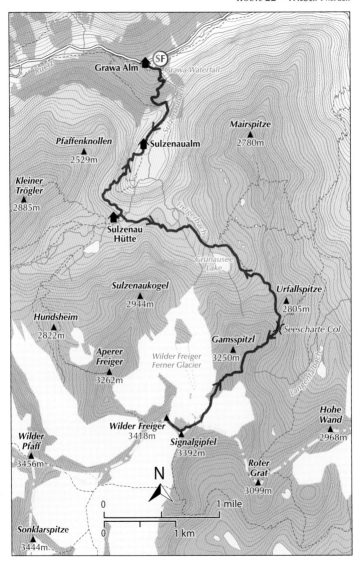

The Sulzenauhütte in the distance

Sulzenauhütte (tel 0664 2716898, **www.sulzenauhuette.at**, open early June until end of September), run by the same family for four generations, is a perfect sun trap and one of the main bases for mountain activities in the Stubai Alps.

Ascent
1300m ascent, 5hrs

From the Sulzenauhütte head east, following signs for Wilder Frieger and Gamsspitzl, on a path which is initially quite flat but begins to climb gently after 500 metres. Roughly 1km after the hut the path splits with 'Wilder Freiger Leo's Weg' signposted off to the right. Ignore this and keep following signs taking you leftwards towards Gamsspitzl (Leo's Weg is an alternative way to the summit of Wilder Freiger that has become increasingly treacherous due to glacial retreat). After the path split, the route drops then continues to climb up to the beautiful **Grünausee Lake** (2330m), which is reached around 1hr after leaving the hut.

After the lake the path is initially on grass but becomes increasingly rocky as it climbs towards the **Seescharte Col** (2762m). Even when it is rocky and not especially clear underfoot there are still plenty of red and white paint marks to show you the way. The final 100m up to the col are quite steep and feel like hard work but keep going as the stunning view from the col is ample reward for your efforts!

From the col turn right and continue to climb, now on the left-hand side of Gamsspitzl's north east ridge. The climb is rocky and requires short sections of very easy scrambling but a rope is not required and the route is clearly marked with paint marks. As you near the summit of **Gamsspitzl** the path drifts left, away from the summit, so if you want to tag the top, you will have to make a half-hour detour to do so.

From level with the summit of Gamsspitzl, continue following paint marks along the ridge which separates the two most easterly branches of the Wilder Freiger Ferner glacier. Although progress requires concentration, do try and stop occasionally to take in the scenery – this is a truly magnificent place to be.

The ridge leads gently between the two sections of glacier and then broadens and climbs up to the summit ridge of Wilder Freiger. The final section up to the summit ridge is partly on rock and partly on snow/ice. Depending on conditions and the exact route you choose (it can vary depending on whether you prefer rock or snow) crampons might be required. Whichever route you take, cresting the summit ridge is a wonderful feeling, partly because of the huge views across the peaks of the Stubai, Silvretta and Ortler ranges, but also because you know that you are close to the reward for all your efforts up to this point!

Once on the summit ridge, turn right and head for the summit. The ridge takes around 15mins and is not technical but does require the occasional easy scrambling move in an exposed position to reach the summit of **Wilder Freiger**.

Descent
1900m descent, 6hrs 30mins
Descend by the same route.

Wilder Freiger summit ridge

ROUTE 23

Zuckerhütl

Start/Finish	Schaufeljoch Col station on the Stubai lift
Ascent	700m
Grade	PD+
Time	2 days (day 1 – 1hr, day 2 – 7–9hrs)
Terrain	Glacier travel, rock scrambling
High point	3507m
Maps	Kompass Map 83 Stubaier Alpen
Public transport	A regular bus service runs directly from Innsbruck to the Stubai ski area.
Access and parking	From Innsbruck follow the A13 for 10km then take exit 10 to Stubaier Gletscher (toll booth) and keep right at the fork to join the B183. Follow this for 29km to the end of the valley to reach the large parking area for the Stubai Glacier lift system. Ride the cable cars up to the Schaufeljoch Col. If the final lift required to get here (Schaufeljoch cable car) is closed, it is possible to walk up from the Stubai Gletscher mid-station (2885m) in 1hr.
Hut	Hildesheimer Hütte
Equipment	Crampons, axe, harness, 30m rope, crevasse rescue equipment, helmet

The Zuckerhütl, 'Sugarloaf' translated into English, gets its name from its distinctive conical shape. It is the highest peak in the Stubai Alps, therefore making it a very popular summit, especially for those wishing to complete the 'Stubai 7 Summits' challenge. Thanks to the Stubai Gletscher lift system at the end of the valley, an ascent of the Zuckerhütl is possible in one day for the fit and acclimatised, however, most climbers prefer to spend a night in the hut and continue to Zuckerhütl the next day, not least to ensure they do not miss the last lift down! The height gain is minimal for the rewards reaped, and the views from the top are awesome. A very worthy summit for anyone's list.

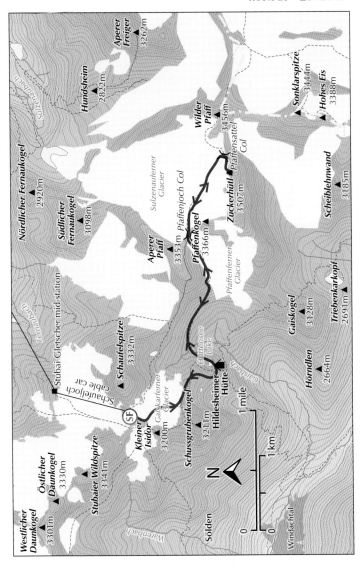

Westlicher Daunkogel 3301m
Östlicher Daunkogel 3330m
Stubaier Wildspitze 3341m
Nördlicher Fernaukogel 2920m
Südlicher Fernaukogel 3098m
Aperer Freiger 3262m
Hundsheim 2822m
Wilder Pfaff 3456m
Sonklarspitze 3444m
Hohes Eis 3388m
Pfaffensattel Col
Aperer Pfaff
Pfaffenkogel 3366m
Zuckerhütl 3507m
Scheiblehnwand 3185m
Pfaffenjoch Col 3353m
Sulzenauferner Glacier
Pfaffenferner Glacier
Schaufelspitze 3332m
Stubai Gletscher mid-station
Gaiskogel 3128m
Triebenkarkopf 2691m
Hörndlen 2664m
Schaufeljoch cable car
Stubai Gletscher mid-station
SF
Kleiner Isidor
Gaiskarferner Glacier 3200m
Schusgrubenkogel 3211m
Müllerhütte lake
Hildesheimer Hütte
Sölden
Windachtal

N

1 mile
1 km
0

131

Approach
250m descent, 1hr
From the **Schaufeljoch** (3150m) walk downhill for 1hr, firstly on what is left of the **Gaiskarferner Glacier** and then on a well-marked trail through glacial moraine, to reach the **Hildesheimer Hütte** (2899m). The hut can also be reached via a very long uphill hike from the town of Sölden in the Ötztal Valley for those not wishing to use a lift.

> Built at the end of the 19th century and surrounded by no less than seven 3000m peaks, Hildesheimer Hütte (tel 05254 2300, **www.hildesheimer huette.at**, 20 bunk beds, 56 mattresses on the floor, open mid/end June until mid/end September) is an environmentally friendly hut, largely powered by solar panels.

Ascent
Descent 100m, ascent 700m, 3–4hrs
From the hut, head north east past the **Hüttensee lake** and descend to a stream via a section of cables. Cross the stream on a wooden bridge and follow paint marks uphill through moraine to reach the foot of the **Pfaffenferner Glacier**. Don crampons, rope up (there is crevasse danger from here onwards) and climb up to the **Pfaffenjoch Col** (3212m), which is the boundary between the Pfaffenferner and Sulzenauferner glaciers. Cross onto the **Sulzenauferner Glacier** and make a long ascending traverse south east to reach the **Pfaffensattel Col** (3344m) which lies between the Wilder Pfaff peak and Zuckerhütl itself.

Turn right (west) and continue climbing up snow to reach the foot of Zuckerhütl's rocky summit tower. Following red paint marks, scramble up, initially on the east ridge and then, higher up, on the south face, to the summit of **Zuckerhütl** (3507m). The final scramble is not difficult but it is exposed in places and the rock quality can be poor. It is 'only' grade 2 scrambling but those not accustomed to exposed scrambling will find it intimidating and might well be glad of a rope.

Optional additional summits
For those with the time and energy, it is also possible to tag on the Wilder Pfaff peak (3456m) in a 1hr 30min round trip from the Pfaffensattel Col after descending from Zuckerhütl. Climbing to the summit of **Wilder Pfaff** involves no scrambling, just some steepish (30-degree) walking up the easterly part of the Sulzenauferner Glacier, for which crampons will be essential.

Descending from Zuckerhütl summit

Descent
700m descent, ascent 350m, 4–5hrs

Descend via your ascent route. In years past it was possible to descend the Sulzenauferner Glacier and then cross the Beiljoch Col to reach the Dresdner Hütte in the middle of Stubai Gletscher ski area, but this is now impossible as glacial retreat has made the toe of the Sulzenauferner Glacier very dangerous and prone to rockfall. Many online route descriptions still describe this as the descent from Zuckerhütl, hence mentioning it here: do not attempt this route.

ROUTE 24

Wildspitze

Start/Finish	Vent
Ascent	1860m, or 1400m from Stablein
Grade	F+/PD
Time	2 days (1 day – 1hr 30mins or 3hrs, day 2 – 8–9hrs)
Terrain	An interesting variety of well-maintained alpine paths, scree and moraine, and snow and glacier hiking
High point	3772m
Maps	Alpenvereinskarte 30/6 Ötztaler Alpen Wildspitze or Kompass Map 43 Ötztaler Alpen – Otztal – Pitztal
Public transport	Vent is not easily accessible from Innsbruck, but it is possible to take a train from Innsbruck to Ötztal, then a bus to Sölden. From Sölden there is a direct bus which goes to the lift station in Vent and takes around 30mins.
Access and parking	Continue through the ski town of Sölden and after 4km along the B186 take the right-hand turning signposted for Vent. Some 14km later you will arrive in the small village of Vent. Park in the lift station parking area.
Hut	Breslauer Hütte
Equipment	Harness, helmet, 30m glacier rope, crampons, ice axe, crevasse rescue equipment

At 3772m, the Wildspitze is the highest peak in the region of Tirol, and the second highest in Austria. The overall climb is enjoyable, varied and well worth the effort for the views from the superb summit. The ascent takes two days, split by a night at the Breslauer Hütte. The route from the hut to the summit is not difficult, but it does cross some fairly serious glaciated terrain so taking a mountain guide is advisable if you are not an experienced mountaineer. As an overall route the rewards are excellent and requires minimal effort to reach such a fantastic peak.

Approach
480m ascent, 1hr 30mins from Stablein or 940m ascent, 3hrs from Vent
From Vent, there is a good walking track up to the restaurant or you can take the chairlift, saving yourself 460m of ascent, to reach the **Stablein restaurant**.

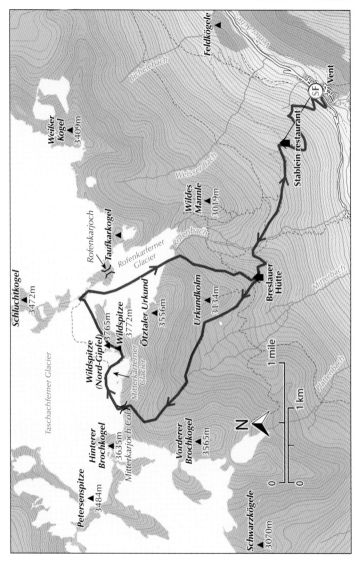

Stablein restaurant, tel 05254 30128, is a cosy self service eatery with wonderful panoramic views.

From here follow the walking sign for the Breslauer Hütte, allowing 1hr 30mins for the ascent along a well-maintained yet fairly steep hiking trail.

The Breslauer Hütte (tel 0676 9634596, **www.breslauerhuette.at**, 67 bunk beds, 99 mattresses on the floor, open mid June until end of September) is actually a small collection of buildings, picturesque and welcoming, providing food and drinks as well as a bed for the night. An ideal sun spot with unrivalled mountain views as far as the eye can see, it is popular with day trippers and mountaineers aiming to climb the Wildspitze.

Extension via Wildes Mannle
Those wishing to extend the walk can take a path off to the right 30mins after leaving the chairlift, signposted 'Breslauer Hütte über Wildes Mannle' (2hrs 30mins). At 3019m, Wildes Mannle is a great summit in its own right, providing a bit of acclimatisation and a way of adding another 3000m summit to your trip.

Ascent
930m ascent, 4–5hrs
From the **Breslauer Hütte**, take the hiking trail which continues behind the main building, where Wildspitze über Mitterkarjoch is signposted as 3hrs 45mins

Setting off up the moraine field

away. Follow a pleasant path, climbing gently and well marked with red and white paint, until you reach a moraine field. Here the path becomes less clear but continues to wind gradually upwards without gaining too much height, now following a series of cairns rather than paint marks and heading for what remains of the **Mitterkarferner Glacier**. Once directly underneath the Mitterkarjoch Col, the route starts to bear right, across much more snowy ground, towards a snow-filled gully. Continue up this gully, (crampons may be required) until it starts to narrow, and you will see some fixed cables attached to the rock on your left. Follow this short, enjoyable grade B via ferrata, which brings you to the **Mitterkarjoch Col**, an outstanding location with a stunning view across the Taschachferner Glacier. Allow 2½–3hrs for the ascent from the hut to the col.

From here on is glaciated terrain, so full glacier kit and roping up is necessary. You also have a fantastic view of the Wildspitze itself, so the end is in sight! Cross over the col and bear round to the right, initially descending slightly, followed by a long traverse and a 20min ascent up to a small col at the bottom of a rocky scramble at the south ridge of the peak. The final 50m is a scramble up the ridge, following a muddy, rocky path to reach the summit cross on **Wildspitze**.

Descent
1405m descent, 4hrs
The descent route described here is more difficult terrain than if you were to take the same route back, but it has the advantage of providing a round trip. Follow the snowy ridge north east off the summit and over two slightly lower peaks (3765m and 3677m). In between these peaks there is an exposed descent down a snowy ridge which requires excellent cramponning technique and a good head for heights. After the second peak walk easily to the col at 3552m which overlooks the Rofenkarferner Glacier. Traverse around the small rocky summit north of the col and descend a rocky ridge towards the Rofenkarjoch (col). After 50 metres on the rocky ridge the **Rofenkarferner Glacier** can be easily accessed. Go down the glacier's right-hand side for 1km until it starts to peter out and give way to rock. Follow a series of cairns along an increasingly distinctive path which eventually leads back to the **Breslauer Hütte**. Allow 3hrs from the summit to the hut. Then continue on the same path as you ascended, passing the Stablein restaurant, to return to **Vent**.

🪨 SPORT CLIMBING

*Climbing the slabs at Achensee
(Route 28)*

Rock climbing is an integral part of life in Austria. Its roots in Tirol can be traced back over 100 years and indeed some of the best climbers and boulderers competing on the world stage have hailed from Innsbruck. Tirol has a reputation for being a tough climbing destination, which is not unfounded as it does boast some of the best and most difficult sport climbing in the world. However, it is not only for the experienced and bold climbers, there is a huge variety of choice from easy to mid-grades, suitable for families, children and beginners, all the way up to those seemingly impossible grade 8 and 9s.

Routes are graded according to the French sports grading system, from grade 3 upwards, with the numbers always accompanied by a letter: 'a' is easier than 'c' so, for example, grade 5a is easier than a 5b or 5c.

With diverse terrain and an interesting mixture of rock types, the climbing in Tirol ranges from cragging and bouldering to multi-pitch routes, and from via ferrata to ice climbing. All of the sport climbing areas included in this guide are fully bolted, so no extra equipment is needed. It goes without saying that a harness, climbing shoes and a helmet are essential for any climbing activity, as well as a belay device, a chalk bag, karabiners and a couple of slings, but please check which length of rope and how many quickdraws are required for each individual area in 'Equipment' in the information boxes for each route.

There are a number of indoor climbing venues around Innsbruck, including the 'Kletterzentrum', opened in 2017, with over 500 climbing routes and 200 bouldering problems. Of course, climbing can be a very dangerous sport if you do not

The lovely, quiet, secluded gorge of Arzbergklamm (Route 25)

have the necessary skills or experience to deal with ropes and climbing equipment so, if you are new to climbing, consider taking a lesson beforehand, always take either a guide or a more experienced climbing partner with you, and never try anything you do not feel comfortable with.

Included here are six of the most easily accessible, fun and varied sport climbing areas, suitable for low- to mid-grade climbers. Many of these crags are large areas with a huge number of possible climbing routes, including some much tougher grades, however just a selection of crags and sectors are covered here, aimed at the non-expert, hobby climbers. *Sport Climbing in Tirol* by Vertical Life is a bilingual guidebook in both English and German and provides a comprehensive guide to sport climbing in Tirol should you wish to tackle an area in more detail.

ROUTE 25

Arzbergklamm

Start	Near Telfs
Grade	3–7a+
Time	10min walk-in
Maps	Kompass Map 36 Innsbruck Brenner or Map 036 Innsbruck und Umgebung
Access and parking	From Innsbruck follow the A12 west for 16km and take the exit for Telfs Ost. At the roundabout go straight on in the direction of Seefeld and pass a petrol station on the right. At the next roundabout take the third exit signposted 'Telfs Zentrum' and after 700 metres turn right at numerous green signs, one of which points uphill in the direction of Tennisanlage. Turn right again immediately onto Birkenberg Straße, still following signs for Tennisanlage. Continue uphill past a church and a post office on the right, then immediately before the bridge to the tennis courts, the road bends to the left and leads to the parking area for the climbing crags. There is room here for around eight cars.
Equipment	50m rope and 12 quickdraws

From the parking area, follow the road which soon turns into a path and quickly brings you to the start of the gorge. There are several separate climbing areas in the gorge, all individually signposted, the first of which will soon appear on the left-hand side. The two sectors featured here – Plattenfuchs and Staustufenwandl – contain some of the lower grades and are easily identified on the right-hand side of the gorge. The two 'Höhlensektor' areas feature further low-grade routes, including several multi-pitch routes, and can be found in between Plattenfuchs and Staustufenwandl.

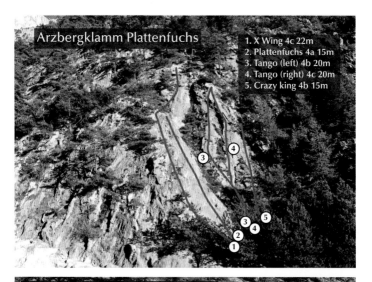

Arzbergklamm Plattenfuchs

1. X Wing 4c 22m
2. Plattenfuchs 4a 15m
3. Tango (left) 4b 20m
4. Tango (right) 4c 20m
5. Crazy king 4b 15m

Arzbergklamm Staustufenwandl

1. Mouse club 4a 8m
2. Strolchi 4a 8m
3. Ace of Hearts (1st pitch) 5b 20m
4. Ace of Hearts (2nd pitch) 5c 10m
5. Raindrops 6a 10m

Summary of the area

Arzbergklamm is a beautiful, secluded little sport climbing area, suitable for all abilities from beginner to advanced. The crags are positioned on either side of a small river, and the picturesque views out of the mouth of the gorge make for a lovely, relaxed day climbing. Most of these quiet routes are short and slabby, but many can be linked to create multi-pitch routes, with some further options for bouldering in the forest.

 ROUTE 26

OeAV klettergarten

Start	Near Martinsbühel
Grade	3–7b
Time	10min walk-in
Maps	Kompass Map 36 Innsbruck Brenner or Map 036 Innsbruck und Umgebung
Access and parking	From Innsbruck take the B171 west and once past the airport you will pass the Innsbruck Kranebitten Camping. Five kilometres further, on the right, you will see the small parking area for the OeAV klettergarten, with space for around 10 cars.
Equipment	60m rope and eight quickdraws

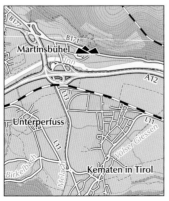

Access to the crag

Follow the path out of the back of the car park and into the forest for 100 metres to reach a series of yellow signs. Take the right-hand path where 'AV-Klettergarten' is signposted. You will pass a very small slab with a few short routes on it and soon after reach a junction with two more yellow signs, directing you to either the left (linker Teil) or right (rechter Teil) sides of the main sector, although once at the wall, these sectors merge together and you can walk between them. The topo in this guide shows the 24 routes

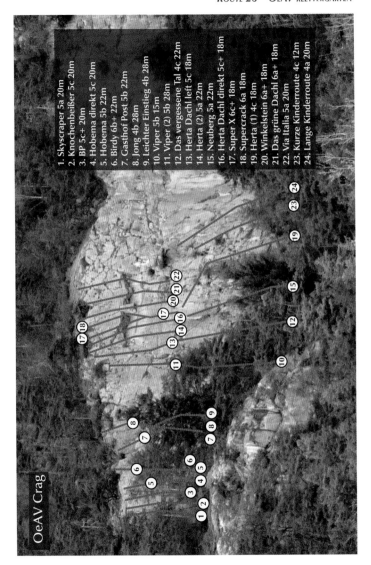

OeAV Crag

1. Skyscraper 5a 20m
2. Knochenbeißer 5c 20m
3. BP 5c+ 20m
4. Hobema direkt 5c 20m
5. Hobema 5b 22m
6. Birdy 6b+ 22m
7. Gasthof Post 5b 22m
8. Jong 4b 28m
9. Leichter Einstieg 4b 28m
10. Viper 5b 15m
11. Viper (2) 5b 28m
12. Das vergessene Tal 4c 22m
13. Herta Dachl left 5c 18m
14. Herta (2) 5a 22m
15. Neuberg 5a 22m
16. Herta Dachl direkt 5c+ 18m
17. Super X 6c+ 18m
18. Supercrack 6a 18m
19. Herta (1) 4c 18m
20. Winkelstein 6a+ 18m
21. Das grüne Dachl 6a+ 18m
22. Via Italia 5a 20m
23. Kurze Kinderroute 4c 12m
24. Lange Kinderroute 4a 20m

143

on the left-hand sector, a further 30 routes can be found on the right-hand side, graded 4a to 7b.

Summary of the area
The OeAV klettergarten is the official crag of the Austrian Alpine Club (OeAV). Of the numerous climbing areas that can be found on the impressive Martinswand wall, OeAV is one of the easiest and most accessible crags. The slabs of rock are quite steep and polished. The climbing is varied, with over 50 routes across the main sector, all on limestone and none of them longer than 30m, with several options for multi-pitch additions. The crags are hidden in the trees and make for a very picturesque and peaceful setting.

 ROUTE 27

Engelswand

Start	Near Tumpen
Grade	3–8a+
Time	5min walk-in
Maps	Kompass Map 35 Imst – Telfs – Kühtai – Mieminger Kette or Map 36 Innsbruck Brenner
Access and parking	A kilometre south of Tumpen, the crag will appear across the fields on the left-hand side of the valley. Take a left turn directly opposite a bus stop, signposted for the Engelswand climbing area as well as 'Lehn and Platzl'. Park in the designated pay and display parking area for Engelswand.
Equipment	60m rope and eight quickdraws

Access to the crag
You will be able to see the crag from the car park, just a 5min walk along the road. Detailed here are a number of the easier grade routes on the far right-hand side of the wall.

Summary of the area
A really beautiful location for a climbing crag, and just 45mins drive from Innsbruck in the lovely Ötztal Valley, Engelswand is understandably very popular, especially at the weekends. Set at the edge of a beautiful meadow in a sunny

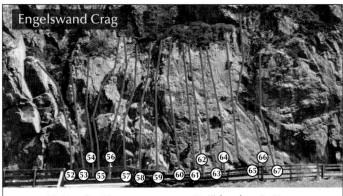

Engelswand Crag

52. Maus 5a+ 18m	60. Kichererbsen 5a 22m
53. Himmel und Hölle 5b 18m	61. Fräulein Fingerwinkel 5a 25m
54. Gräfin 4c 18m	62. Buschräuber 5a 25m
55. Frühstücksei 4a 18m	63. Minidream 5c 25m
56. Hopp oder Drop 4b 18m	64. Polenta alla Monte 5c 25m
57. Ötzis Weg 4a 20m	65. Echt cool 5b 25m
58. Lucky Luke 3c 20m	66. Für Reini 5b 20m
59. Kasperltheater 4b 22m	67. Dampfnudel 6b 20m

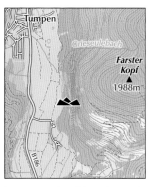

About as civilised as sport climbing gets

location, with public toilets and a picnic area, it is very much suited to families and casual climbers. There are more than 70 granite routes ranging from easy grade 3s up to more challenging 7s and 8s, but with 20 routes under grade 6 there really is something to suit all abilities. Several of the routes have name labels at the bottom, making it easy to find the one you are looking for, and there is also an information board at the bottom of the crag with a very comprehensive topo showing all the routes, including names and grades. With such a picturesque setting and a flat approach of just 5mins, Engelswand is a great choice for a relaxed and stress-free day of climbing.

 ROUTE 28

Rofan cragging, Achensee

Start	Top station of the Rofan cable car
Grade	3–6b
Time	25–30min walk-in
Maps	Kompass Map 027 Achensee
Access and parking	From Innsbruck follow the A12 eastwards for 34km and take exit Wiesing to merge onto Achensee Straße B181 and follow this winding road for 9km to reach the Rofan cable car on the right-hand side. Take this cable car up to the top.
Equipment	50m rope and eight quickdraws

Access to the crags
Grubastiege – From the cable car station, walk north for 5mins on a large path to reach the Mauritzalm Hütte. Immediately behind the hut the path splits. Take the right-hand branch in the direction of Rofanspitze and follow this for 10mins until it passes under a series of very broken, grassy cliffs and begins to ascend. After 7–8mins of climbing, the path flattens out and the crag is on the left, 5 metres off the path.

Platzl – From the Grubastiege crag, continue along the path for another couple of mins as it climbs a small rise. At the top of the rise the path flattens out briefly and the crag is visible on the right, 50 metres away. Follow a tiny and easy-to-miss path to the foot of the routes.

Summary of the area
Climbers looking for superb limestone with unbeatable views will be hard pushed to find better than the numerous crags available at the top of the Rofan lift, set

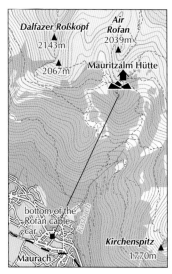

high above the stunning Lake Achensee. The landscape and scenery in the Rofan area is truly spectacular, and the various crags cater for all climbing abilities from routes suitable for families and small children, up to much more challenging grade 7s and 8s. In general, the routes are short and slabby, but the crags are close together, meaning you can cover a lot of ground in a day. There are nine areas in total, accessible from the top of the lift. Listed here are two of the easiest crags, with routes ranging from grade 3 up to grade 6.

The sectors

Grubastiege – A warm, sunny crag which dries quickly, this is an excellent little area, ideal for a half day of low grade

Rofan Crags Grubastiege

1. Mickey Mouse 4a 7m
2. Robin Hood 4a 7m
3. Goofy 5a 7m
4. Spider man 5b 7m
5. Pinocchio 5c 7m
6. Snoopy 3a 6m
7. Bart Simpson 2 6m

Rofan Crags Platzl (left)

1. Die Direkte 6b 10m
2. Mike extreme 3 10m
3. Rampenfuehre 5a 10m
4. Schwarze Verschneidung 5a 10m

Rofan Crags Platzl (right)

5. Samira 6a+ 8m
6. Valentin 6a 8m

ticking or for bringing the family. The views across the peaks of the Karwendel range are stunning. Although short, the routes are excellent and exceptionally well bolted.

Platzl – A fun little crag, this is well worth stopping at on the way to or from Grubaplatte. The crag sits in a small dip and receives a lot of sun with very little wind. As such it dries quickly and is usually warmer than other crags in the area.

Grubaplatte – This area is not covered here but is just a short walk from Platzl and also well worth a visit. A slab lovers' paradise, Grubaplatte is home to low-mid grade routes, ideal for practising precise footwork. The crag is slightly more sheltered than Platzl and Grubastiege but still sees plenty of sun and is usually dry after half a day of good weather.

ROUTE 29

Klettergarten Oetz

Start	Oetz
Grade	3–7c
Time	30sec walk-in
Maps	Kompass Map 35 Imst – Telfs – Kühtai – Mieminger Kette or Map 36 Innsbruck Brenner
Access and parking	From Innsbruck follow the A12 west for 50km. Take exit 123 towards Ötztal and Haiming. Continue along the B186 for 1km to reach a roundabout, go straight across and after a further 3.5km the crag will appear on the left-hand side along with a small parking area, signposted as 'P klettergarten'. This is just to the left of the builders' merchants 'Franz Thurner' and just before the road sign welcoming you into Oetz
Equipment	60m rope and eight quickdraws

Summary of the area

This is an excellent granite climbing area on the outskirts of the village of Oetz in the beautiful Ötztal Valley, just over 40mins' drive from Innsbruck. It is an ideal crag for beginners due to the number of easy routes, but also popular with more ambitious climbers with many more difficult routes. The routes in general are quite polished and steep and

149

Klettergarten Oetz

1. Fidibus 3 20m
2. Schlumpf 3 20m
— 1 & 2

3. Maus 3 20m
4. Bandit 4 20m
5. Sonneln 5 25m
6. Küken 3 15m
7. Lauser 5+ 15m
8. Klein aber oho 6a 5m
9. Flying Power 6a+ 5m
10. Spätherbst 6a 30m
11. Flügel 6a+ 30m
12. Guater Haggen 6b 30m
13. Amor - 6a 30m
14. Bizeps 6a 30m
15. Kante 5c 20m
16. Linke Rampe 5b 20m
17. Rechte Rampe 5b 20m

Climbing the slabs at Klettergarten Oetz

get progressively harder the further right you move along the crag, so the topo in this guide covers the first 20 routes, starting from the left-hand side of the wall. All the route names are clearly labelled at the start of each route and at the entrance to the crag there is a very comprehensive topo of the area complete with a diagram, route names and grades, making for a stress-free and enjoyable day climbing.

With a walk-in of less than a minute, shady trees and picnic benches, it is hard to find any negatives! It is located next to a road, but the traffic noise does not detract from the enjoyment of the climbing. The rock is south facing so lovely and sunny, and it has over 40 routes to suit all abilities. Despite all this, it is rarely busy, and it can be easily combined with a visit to nearby Piburgesee (Route 60) for an afternoon or evening swim.

ROUTE 30

Emmentaler multi-pitch

Start	Near Martinsbühel
Grade	5a
Time	20min walk-in
Maps	Kompass Map 36 Innsbruck Brenner or Map 036 Innsbruck und Umgebung
Access and parking	From Innsbruck take the B171 west and once past the airport you will pass the Innsbruck Kranebitten Camping. Five kilometres further, on the right, you will see the small parking area for the OeAV klettergarten, with space for around 10 cars.
Equipment	60m rope, 13 quickdraws, helmet

Emmentaler

1. 4b 45m
2. 4b 40m
3. 5a 35m
4. 4c 45m

● = belays

Access to the crag

Follow the path up from the end of the parking area into the trees. After 2mins you come to a yellow sign. Turn left and 20 metres later go right at another yellow sign. Both the signs are signposted 'Martinswand Vorbau Routen'. Follow the path steeply up through the trees for just over 10mins to emerge at the foot of 'Emmentaler', which is marked with a metal plaque.

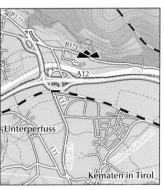

Summary of the area

Part of the mighty Martinswand climbing area on the outskirts of Innsbruck, Emmentaler is one of the easiest multi-pitch routes on the main face. This is a really fun, mostly grade 4 route with one section of grade 5, on fantastic rock in a superb location. The four pitches provide 2hrs of enjoyable climbing.

Descent

From the top of Emmentaler, follow red dots diagonally up and across broken ledges at the top of the crag. It feels somewhat counterintuitive to go up at the start of the descent, but after 5–10mins of slightly exposed ledge crossings, the path becomes more distinct and begins to descend. Follow it down onto a short scree slope then past the Alpinmagazin crag and back into the trees, where it eventually joins the approach path. Allow 30mins for the descent.

ⓖ Via ferratas

The rope bridge on the Innsbrucker klettersteig (Route 31)

Via ferratas (known as *klettersteig* in German) are fixed rope routes which provide an alternative to traditional rock climbing and are, for many, a fantastic way of being able to climb in the mountains without needing experience or expertise in rope work or belaying. Via ferratas (which first appeared in the Italian Dolomites during World War I to enable soldiers to travel safely through the mountains) are becoming increasingly popular across the Alps, and now in Tirol alone there are over 100 routes. Within a short drive of Innsbruck, a large number of via ferratas can be found, with varying degrees of difficulty.

Via ferratas are graded as A–E, with A being the easiest and suitable for children or complete beginners. The most challenging grade is E, which is categorised as extremely difficult and physical. These often feature sustained steep, overhanging sections requiring a great deal of upper body strength and stamina, and should not be undertaken lightly. The views from the summits are almost always spectacular and well worth the effort.

Via ferratas can vary from easy one-hour routes to full day, or even multi-day, routes traversing a whole mountain range. The routes are secured with steel cables, metal staples and, occasionally, ladders and exciting rope bridges. The permanent presence of the steel cable means that route finding is never a problem, and you are secured to the mountain at all times with your harness and lanyards. However, this should not be mistaken for complete security as, despite being attached to the cable, with several metres between change-over points, it is a long way to fall should you lose your grip, or nerve, and could result in serious injury. Clinging on to a cliff, with several hundred metres of air below, you can feel incredibly exposed and it can be very intimidating. It is important to remember that having set off on a route, it is often very difficult to reverse it; it is best to start with an easy grade to see how you get on before taking on anything more difficult. Both the grading and the length of the routes should therefore be adhered to very carefully, and you should only attempt routes that you are confident you can tackle.

High above the valley on the Geierwand klettersteig (Route 36)

For every via ferrata, whatever the grade, you will need a harness, helmet, gloves, grippy shoes and CE-certified via ferrata lanyards.

ROUTE 31

Innsbrucker klettersteig

Start	Top station (Hafelekar) of the Hungerburg lift
Finish	Mid-station (Seegrube) of the Hungerburg lift
Grade	C
Time	4–5hrs for the first section (10min walk-in; 3–4hrs climbing, a 45min walk-down) or 6½–8hrs for both sections (10min walk-in; 3–4hrs for the first section, walk 20mins to second section and 2hrs to complete, a 1–1hr 30min walk-down)
Maps	Kompass Map 36 Innsbruck Brenner or Map 036 Innsbruck und Umgebung
Public transport	The easiest option is to go by public transport. Take the bus or funicular railway from Innsbruck centre to the Hungerburg cable car station. From the Hungerburg station, take the Nordkette cable car to Hafelekar (the highest station). See below for directions to the klettersteig.
Access and parking	It is possible to drive directly up to Hungerburg and park at the lift station. From the Hungerburg station, take the Nordkette cable car to Hafelekar (the highest station).
Note	The signs say that the approach takes 15mins but in reality it is more like 5–10mins. There is a copper sign marking the start of the route.

The wonderful Innsbrucker klettersteig makes for a classic day out on a stunning alpine ridge high above Innsbruck city centre. The first section is often done on its own but the second part, although slightly tougher, is excellent and well worth doing. The views across the wild and remote peaks of the Karwendel are superb throughout.

Access to the via ferrata
From Hafelekar, follow the large and well-signposted path west to the foot of the klettersteig, which begins just north of a small weather station building.

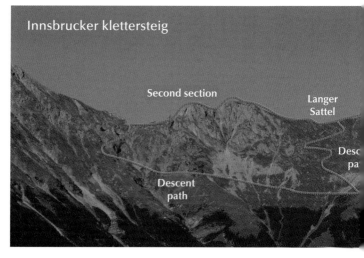

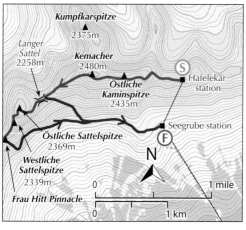

First section

The first 30m of the klettersteig (B/C) are steep but after this the angle eases off and the route becomes an enjoyable scramble. After the first summit, descend to a small notch which looks down a steep north-facing gully then follow a clear path on the south side of the ridge across two wide gullies. There is no cable to protect the path but it is walking terrain rather than scrambling. After the gullies is a col, where the via ferrata resumes. It follows easy (A/B) but occasionally exposed terrain on the ridge crest to the summit of the **Östliche Kaminspitze** (2435m), which is marked by a large cross. Continue along the easy and enjoyable ridge to a very

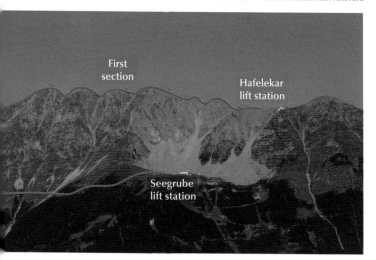

small notch then move onto the north side of the ridge and climb a 10m wall (B) before rejoining the ridge and following it to another summit. Continue along the ridge over more easy terrain, including a fun 5-metre suspension bridge, to the summit of **Kemacher** (2480m). Descend the ridge down to the **Langer Sattel** (2258m) which is exposed and occasionally tricky (B/C).

Descent

From the saddle it is possible to follow a good path for 45mins back to the **Seegrube** cable car station or alternatively follow the directions below to continue to the second section of the via ferrata.

Second section

If you wish to continue to the next section, walk uphill for 20–30mins on a good but steep zig-zag path to reach the **Östliche Sattelspitze** (2369m), where the second section of klettersteig begins. From the summit of the Östliche Sattelspitze, traverse left for 20 metres to reach the top of a steep and somewhat intimidating gully where the cables begin. Descend this (B/C) for 100 metres and exit it leftwards before re-climbing onto a ridge crest. Continue along the ridge crest (B/C) over, under and around some spectacular limestone towers to reach the summit of **Westliche Sattelspitze** (2339m) which is marked with a cross and a plaque. Allow 45–50mins from the Östliche Sattelspitze to the Westliche Sattelspitze.

High above Innsbruck on the Innsbrucker klettersteig

From the cross, descend the ridge leading west towards the spectacular **Frau Hitt pinnacle** (apparently named after a notoriously greedy local land owner who refused to share her wealth and provisions during a famine and was turned to stone as punishment). The final section of descent down to the pinnacle is steep and sustained (C) but great fun.

Descent
From the end of the cables, descend on the north side of Frau Hitt to the col just west of the pinnacle. From here, descend a good path back to **Seegrube** in 1–1hr 30mins.

ROUTE 32

Achensee 5 Gipfel

Start/Finish	Top station of the Rofan-seilbahn cable car, Maurach
Grade	D
Time	6hrs 15mins (1hr walk-in, 4hrs 30mins climbing, 45min walk-down)
Maps	Kompass Map 027 Achensee
Public transport	It is possible to reach Maurach via a train from Innsbruck to Jenbach, changing here for a bus to Maurach.
Access and parking	From Innsbruck follow the A12 east for 30km and take exit 43, signposted 'Jenbach'. Go left at the roundabout and follow Achenseestraße for 4.8km to reach a junction with the B181. Turn left and the cable car station is 250 metres further along on the right, opposite the tourist office. The Rofan-seilbahn car park provides ample parking, especially out of high season.

One of the longest and best via ferratas in the area, this superb route traverses a stunning ridge line, taking in no less than five peaks (hence the name) which tower over the beautiful Achensee Lake and the quaint ski area of Maurach. Taking a full day, the 5 Gipfel strikes a perfect balance between hiking, climbing and scrambling with each summit rewarding you with unbeatable 360-degree panoramas. Each section is independent, enabling an easy escape at various points if time is running short.

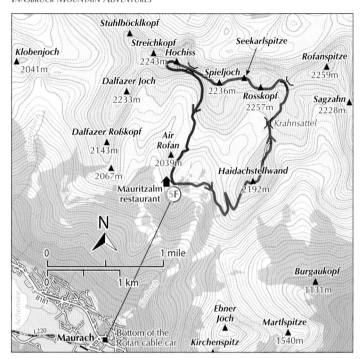

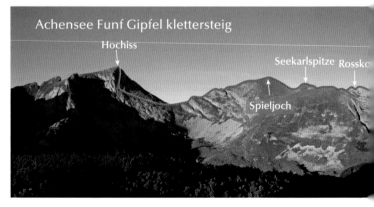

160

Heading for the Hochiss on the 5 Gipfel

Access to the via ferrata

From the top of the lift head for the **Mauritzalm restaurant** and after 100 metres take the right-hand fork, directly below the restaurant, signposted 'Haidachstellwand'. Follow this path as it winds at first towards the first rock buttress of the via ferrata, then briefly away from it before doubling back to reach the foot of the first pitch, which is just to the right of the ridge.

Haidachstellwand

The route

Follow a short section of grade B via ferrata for 10mins then walk easily onto the summit of the **Haidachstellwand**. Descend the ridge on an exposed section of B/C down-climbing northwards to reach the **Krahnsattel**. Take the main path across the bowl, heading directly north towards the large orange-coloured rock face of the Rosskopf. After 150 metres you will reach a fence and a signpost, and a small path branches off right, heading uphill. Follow this towards the col that separates the Rosskopf and the Rofanspitze. After 150 metres a vague path branches off left heading directly up steep scree to the foot of the Rosskopf, either take this or continue up to the **col** to then double back round to the start of the route (longer but less steep).

The Rosskopf section begins fairly steep and physical, with some climbing moves necessary, yet with excellent footholds, both natural and man-made. It soon mellows off, providing some fun scrambling onto the summit of **Rosskopf**. An enjoyable descent down the ridge leads to the grassy col separating the Rosskopf from the Seekarlspitze, which provides an excellent lunch spot.

From the col, cross around to the north side of the Seekarlspitze, opposite the huge clean sweep of stunning grey limestone. Traverse for around 100 metres before heading straight up to the most difficult section of the entire route (for a short pitch here the man-made footholds are less generous so some bold moves and a little smearing are required). The last few moves are thoroughly enjoyable and lead to the **Seekarlspitze summit** with another stunning view.

Follow the wide grassy ridge downwards heading for the **Spieljoch** and an easy path leads to the summit. From here, the col separating you from the foot of the Hochiss looks tantalisingly close, yet it is in fact only reached via a steep and exposed section of protected down-scrambling. Once at the **col** you have the option to finish the day here and take the path back towards the cable car, however to tag the final summit, follow the easy path directly towards the south east face of the Hochiss for around 15mins to reach the foot of the wall. A superb final pitch of grade C via ferrata takes you up fantastic limestone runnels (channels) to the summit cross at the top of the **Hochiss**.

Descent

From the summit take the path heading back down towards the cable car, initially veering steeply left before flattening out.

ROUTE 33

Crazy Eddy klettersteig

Start/Finish	Silz
Grade	C or D (two variants)
Time	2hrs 20mins (20min walk-in, 1hr 30mins climbing, 30min walk-down)
Maps	Kompass Map 35 Imst – Telfs – Kühtai – Mieminger Kette
Public transport	The crag is very difficult to reach using public transport; driving is really the only option.
Access and parking	On entering Silz from the east along Tiroler Straße, turn right directly opposite the large pink church onto Widumgasse, and follow this for 850 metres until you cross the River Inn. Pass 'TED's White Descents' on the right-hand side just after the river then, 100 metres later, turn right onto Locherbodenweg. Follow this for 350 metres to cross over the autobahn and reach the small parking area on the left-hand side of the road.

This short and enjoyable via ferrata is perfect for an afternoon or as a quick stop en route to or from Innsbruck. With a minimal walk-in and an easier variant, it is ideal as an introduction to via ferrata or for those who would like a quick burst of fun climbing. The views are stunning and the area holds the sun well into the late afternoon.

Access to the via ferrata
From the parking area there are several signposted routes but take the path leading uphill, signposted to Zwischensimmering. Walk uphill through the woods for 15mins until you reach a junction. The left-hand fork leads to the bottom of the more difficult route (D) whereas the right-hand fork will take you to the foot of the easier variant (B/C).

The route
Both routes run parallel to each other directly up the rock face, around 10 metres apart, with the river and the village of Silz providing a picturesque backdrop.

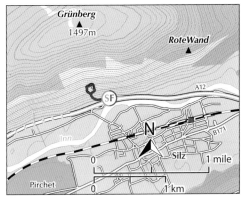

The B/C route involves fun scrambling and steady climbing while the more difficult route requires a little more precision and some trickier moves. After around 15mins climbing, the B/C route reaches an easy path and then a platform, where the two routes converge. Once the routes meet, traverse right for around 10 metres and climb a short section to where the fixed cables run out. Continue uphill bearing left along a narrow path, following the red and white painted markers on the rocks to reach a small clearing where the path splits. Take the right-hand path, following the green 'KL' arrows painted on the rock. The path traverses along the rock face, crossing two very short sections of fixed cables and after the second section you will see a small wooden sign pointing uphill for the

There are not always rungs or staples to help so be prepared to use some rock!

klettersteig. From here you can see the bridge made up of two cables crossing the gully to reach the top of the route. Scramble up to the cables and cross the gully.

Descent

Once you have crossed the bridge, there are two choices for descending. It is possible to abseil from fixed anchors, however, the easier option is to return the direction you came, re-crossing the bridge and following the path back downhill. Where the path splits, follow the left-hand fork downhill, away from the klettersteig, following the red and white paint markers on the rock and bearing left along an easy path. After 20mins the path crosses underneath the rock face. Follow this easy path through the woods to reach the parking area.

ROUTE 34

Peter Kofler klettersteig

Start/Finish	Sankt Jodok
Grade	C
Time	2hrs 50mins (20min walk-in, 1hr 45mins climbing, 45min walk-down)
Maps	Kompass Map 36 Innsbruck Brenner or Map 036 Innsbruck und Umgebung
Public transport	A direct, convenient and very scenic train goes from Innsbruck main train station to Sankt Jodok, and delivers you right to the start of the walk-in.
Access and parking	On reaching the centre of Sankt Jodok, make for the small parking area on the left-hand side of the road, next to the river and opposite the Spar supermarket.
Note	At the top of this route there is wooden chest full of cold soft drinks and beers asking only for a voluntary donation to the mountain rescue association. What a bonus!

This fantastic short via ferrata is in a secluded location so it never gets too busy and finishes at a great little viewpoint. Although it is not too difficult, it is physical enough to get a workout which all in all makes it a perfect afternoon activity or an ideal short stop if travelling between Innsbruck and the Dolomites.

Access to the via ferrata

Cross the river using the bridge between the Raiffeisen bank and the Spar and take the path up to the train station (or start here if you have travelled by train). Pass through the tunnel to the other side of the tracks and turn left to keep following the path, parallel to the railway line. After around 5mins the path drops and it appears that you are going to cross back under the railway but, in fact, it continues on, passing through what initially looks like someone's garden. Finally the path enters a forest and takes a fairly steep course straight up towards the rock face. Follow this for 10mins to reach the foot of the via ferrata.

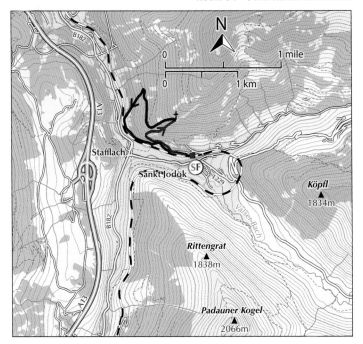

The route

The route begins with a 40m ascent of quite steep ground, which is fairly physical with few metal staples but with chunks chipped out of the rock to provide footholds. This is followed by a long rising traverse to the right to reach a narrow, muddy ledge with quite a distinctive dead tree after 30mins. Ten metres on pass another small ledge with a bench drilled into the wall. From the bench, follow a footpath easily through the woods and after 50 metres you will reach a sign showing 'Aussteig 1' – the first escape route should you require it. After this there is small cable bridge, leading to a horizontal traverse to reach the bottom of an excellent 40m long corridor. This is quite steep but has some nice climbing moves on it and positive footholds all the way. At the top of this is 'Aussteig 2' – the second escape route.

From here you cross a second cable bridge which is a bit more exposed than the last one, then continue on a long, rising traverse up and right across some occasionally steep ground, but generally quite steady. This rising traverse

Peter Kofler klettersteig
St Jodok

Summit
cross

continues easily to the top of the route, to reach a plateau with picnic benches, a **summit cross** with a fantastic view, the obligatory summit book, and the extra bonus of a chest containing cold drinks! Don't forget to leave a donation for the mountain rescue service; this is an excellent organisation.

The wire bridge on the Peter Kofler klettersteig

Descent
From the summit, take the path leading downwards, parallel to the cliff edge. After 10mins you will reach a wooden stile. The path carries on downhill but there is a sign saying 'Kein Abstieg' telling you that you must not descend that way. Cross the stile to join the jeep track and follow this for around 400 metres to reach a small sign pointing left to 'Abstieg Sankt Jodok'. Follow this lovely path through the forest until you reach the railway line. Walk parallel with the railway line, then cross over the tracks to reach **Sankt Jodok**.

ROUTE 35

Ochsenwand/Schlicker klettersteig

Start	Top station (Kreuzjoch) of the Schlick 2000 ski area, Fulpmes
Finish	Mid-station (Froneben) of the Schlick 2000 ski area, Fulpmes
Grade	C/D
Time	7.5hrs (1hr walk-in, 3hrs climbing, 3.5hr walk-down)
Maps	Kompass Map 36 Innsbruck Brenner or Map 036 Innsbruck und Umgebung
Public transport	Fulpmes is easily accessible from Innsbruck via direct bus or train in just over 30mins, or alternatively by using the scenic Stubaital (STB) tram, which takes around 1hr.
Access and parking	Follow signs through the village centre of Fulpmes to reach the large parking area at the foot of the cable car.
Note	From Froneben it is 'only' 300m extra of descent just to walk back down to the car park so this a possibility for those looking to save money.

This is a brilliant route which gives a full day out in the incredibly atmospheric Kalkkögel mountain range and passes through some of the most interesting and unusual rock formations you are ever likely to encounter.

Access to the via ferrata
From the Kreuzjoch cable car station, descend past the Zirmachalm mountain restaurant on a wide and well-signposted path. Continue descending to reach the

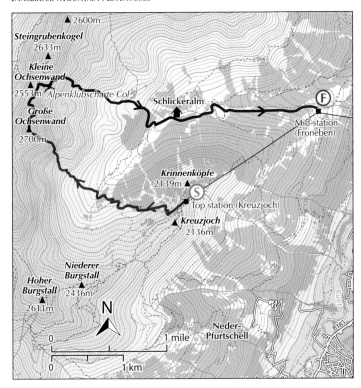

valley that separates the cable car station and the klettersteig. Go across this on a good path to a large information board about the klettersteig. From the information board, follow red paint marks and a path (which is quite vague most of the way) up a scree slope to the foot of the route.

The route

The first 30m of the route, slightly overhanging and physical, is graded C/D but do not be put off – this is the hardest section of the whole day – after this the angle eases off and the next 1hr 30mins are on enjoyable, exposed but never difficult terrain graded between A and C. The route is cleverly designed so as to minimise risk of rockfall by winding left and right, with a rightward leaning ramp after 150m being the only major landmark before a section of steep grass 400m up. Walk up

the steep grass on a good path to reach another short section of cables (B/C) and then another path up more grass. After this second section of grass, follow the broken summit ridge of the Große Ochsenwand over a series of steps. These include some sections of very easy scrambling and a brief section of grade C via ferrata. At the end of them the summit of **Große Ochsenwand** (2700m) awaits and what a summit it is, with wonderful rock architecture and views stretching for miles.

Descent

From the summit, head along the north ridge in the direction of the **Kleine Ochsenwand**. The descent is really enjoyable and takes you along the ridge crest and also off to both sides of the ridge, all the while leading through some fantastic rock formations. The route is well marked with paint marks and there are also some long sections of via ferrata cable (maximum grade C) which allow you to move through some very improbable looking passages.

After 1hr 30mins of descent from the summit, the ridge eventually leads you to the **Alpenklubscharte Col** at 2451m. From here, follow a well signed and clear path for 1hr down to the **Schlickeralm** (1645m).

Schlickeralm (tel 05225 62409, www.schlickeralm.com/de, open daily throughout the summer) is a working farm producing their own milk, butter and cheese.

Impressive rock formations on the Ochsenwand Klettersteig

Have a well-earned drink and then continue down for a further hour to find yourselves back at the the mid-station cable car (Froneben). Ride this back down to the carpark.

ROUTE 36
Geierwand klettersteig

Start/Finish	Haiming
Grade	C
Time	3hrs 45mins (15min walk-in, 2hrs 30mins climbing, 1hr walk-down)
Maps	Kompass Map 35 Imst – Telfs – Kühtai – Mieminger Kette
Public transport	Haiming can be reached via train from Innsbruck, changing once in Ötztal.
Access and parking	From Innsbruck follow the A12 west for 37km then take the exit signposted for Mötz. Go straight across the T-junction at the end of the slip road then take the first turning on the left. Pass under the motorway and follow the road as it swings round 180 degrees to another T-junction. Go left and follow the road for 6km to reach a turn off right, signposted for Haiming, onto the Alte Bundesstraße road. Follow this for 1.5km as it passes to the north of Haiming village to reach a bridge across the River Inn. Go across the bridge and turn immediately right at the far end onto Magerbach. Follow this for 250 metres to a parking area on the right with an information board about the klettersteig and park here.

This excellent via ferrata has sustained interest but without any real difficulty. The route takes a great, clean line up some lovely rock and is long enough to provide a day out in itself, but also short enough that it can be easily combined with Crazy Eddy (Route 33) to give a full day of action.

Access to the via ferrata
Continue on foot along Magerbach for 50 metres to a path leading off left, signposted to the klettersteig. The path goes through a small field then crosses over the motorway before climbing up to the foot of the klettersteig. The marginally tougher start is on the left, the easier version begins on the right, at a small wooden shack.

The route

The left-hand start goes up the slabs of Haiming climbing crag and then a short walking section leads to a horizontal ledge, from where it is possible to traverse into the right-hand start. Above the

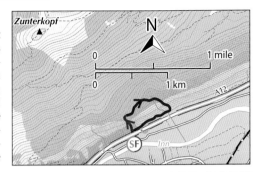

Geierwand klettersteig

Wire bridge

Haiming climbing crag

ledge there is a steep corner (B/C) and 20 metres above this, the two routes converge.

The right-hand start is marginally easier (B) and leads up series of steps and ledges to where the two routes meet. Above here, the route winds gradually to the right up some beautiful grey and orange limestone with sustained B level difficulties and the odd steeper step to a yellow bench, perched high above a deep gully.

Shortly after the bench the route passes into the gully then climbs up to a wire bridge which crosses the gully. Above the bridge there is a steep section and then a short walk to reach a final rising traverse into the trees.

Using the staples on the Geierwand klettersteig

Descent

Follow a clear path down the left-hand side of the cliff (when facing downhill). The path is steep in places and has some short sections of fixed cables to act as handrails, but it is not necessary to clip in at any stage. After 45mins on the path, you reach a jeep track. Turn right and follow this down for 5mins to where it meets the approach path. Follow this for another 5mins to reach the parking area in **Haiming**.

ROUTE 37

Kühtai Panorama klettersteig

Start	Top station of the Dreiseenbahn chairlift, Kühtai
Finish	Alpenrose Hotel, Kühtai
Grade	D/E
Time	4hrs (30min walk-in, 2hrs climbing, 1hr 30min walk-down)
Maps	Kompass Map 35 Imst – Telfs – Kühtai – Mieminger Kette
Public transport	A direct bus will take you directly from Innsbruck to Kühtai. Take the Dreiseenbahn chairlift up.
Access and parking	Pass straight through the village of Kühtai and drop down the other side to soon see the distinctive pink building of the Alpenrose Hotel on the left behind the Dreiseenbahn chairlift. Park here and take the chairlift.
Note	Only a one-way ticket is needed on the Dreiseenbahn chairlift as you will descend via a different route.

One of the more physical and athletic via ferratas in the area, this superb route with outstanding views and interesting and varied terrain, also reaches a fantastic peak where you can celebrate your achievement by signing your name in the obligatory summit book.

The route is divided into two clear parts with a short walk linking them. There are physical sections of grade D on both and a short section of D/E towards the end of part one. The route combines a wide variety of climbing from exposed ridges to vertical walls and a final exciting climb through a chimney to top out at the summit cross of the Pockkogel peak.

From the summit you can enjoy wonderful views over the Stubai and Ötztal alps and across to the Wildspitze. Weather permitting you may even be able to see all the way to the Zugspitze, Germany's highest peak.

Access to the via ferrata

Straight ahead, 50 metres from the top of the **Dreiseenbahn chairlift** you will see a yellow hiking sign directing you up a rocky path towards 'Klettersteig – Einstieg' and 'Pockkogel über Klettersteig'. The sign says 20mins to the start but

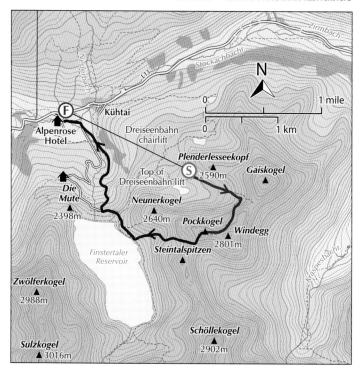

allow 30mins. Follow the red and white paint markers as the path winds upwards initially and eventually turns right to the foot of the route.

The route

Part one begins steadily, soon leading to a steep wall of grade D, quite physical but equipped with a number of metal staples. This then eases off to some enjoyable, gentle climbing, finishing with the crux; a short section of overhanging, physical climbing at grade D/E.

From the top of part one, head right across the boulder field, initially along quite an exposed path and following the signs to the beginning of the second part. During this traverse be sure to maintain the same height and do not be tempted to climb any higher. Traverse around a buttress to reach the foot of part two, marked with a large red paint dot.

Kühtai Panorama klettersteig

Pockkogel

Descent
not visible

Part 2

Part 1

To Dreiseenbahn

Part two is much more varied, initially climbing with some sections of C/D, but flattening off in the latter half to weave along the ridge and traverse towards the summit. After the first fairly steep section be sure to have a rest on the tiny wooden seat which has been fixed to the rock next to a 'Parkplatz' sign; although not for those with a fear of heights! Once the route starts to flatten there is a short down-climb and some ridge scrambling before a thoroughly enjoyable chimney section and a final very short steep section of grade D before reaching the summit cross on **Pockkogel**.

One of the steeper sections on the Kühtai Panorama klettersteig

Descent

The descent path follows the red and white paint markers initially down through a boulder field but soon turns into a clear path. This brings you out at the **Finstertaler**

dam, a beautiful turquoise green reservoir high above Kühtai and well worth a visit in itself. From here follow the easy path back down to the **Alpenrose Hotel** car park.

🕐 ROUTE 38

Absamer klettersteig (plus Westgrat and Eisengattergrat klettersteig)

Start/Finish	Absam
Grade	C
Time	7hrs 45 mins for the single-day option or 11hrs 30mins–12hrs over two days (day 1 – 5hrs 15mins; day 2 – 6hrs 15mins–6hrs 45mins). Day 1 – 1hr 15min walk-in, 4hrs climbing, 2hr 30min descent to the car park (if omitting the second day). Day 2 – 45min walk-in, 2hrs climbing, 3hrs 30min–4hr descent.
Maps	Kompass Map 36 Innsbruck Brenner or Map 036 Innsbruck und Umgebung
Public transport	A direct and regular bus service runs between Innsbruck and Absam, or to get you even closer to the start, you can take a bus to Hall in Tirol then change for a bus to Gnadenwald, getting off at the Bettelwurfsiedlung stop at the entrance to the Halltal.
Access and parking	From Hall in Tirol, take the Salzbergstraße following signs for Absam Gnadenwald. After 3km at the four-way junction continue straight on to Halltal and you will shortly reach the large car park in front of the entrance to the Hall Valley, indicated by a large banner sign welcoming you to the Karwendel: 'Herzlich Willkommen Alpenpark Karwendel'. This is the end of the vehicle access and from here you can only enter the Karwendel on foot.

This is a fantastic long route through a disused coal mine finishing at a superb mountain hut which is positioned underneath the Großer Bettelwurf peak overlooking the town of Hall in Tirol. Staying overnight in the hut is an excellent option as, not only is the location second to none, it also provides a perfect halfway point to link this with the Westgrat and Eisengattergrat klettersteig the following day.

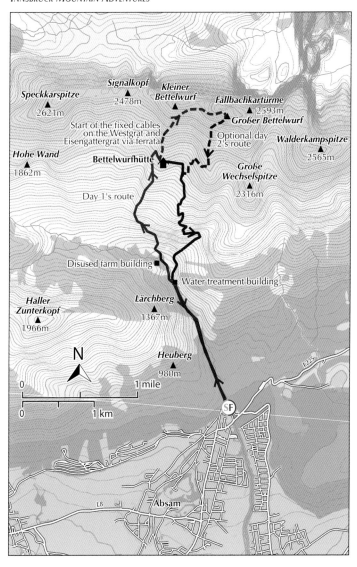

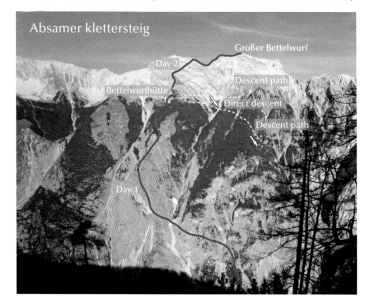

Absamer klettersteig

Großer Bettelwurf

Day 2

Descent path

Bettelwurfhütte

Direct descent

Descent path

Day 1

Access to the via ferrata

From the car park take the road underneath the large sign and follow this for 45mins until you enter a forested area much more densely populated with trees. You will see a **disused farm building** with a green roof on your left. Note – about 20mins before this there is a signpost showing a path to the Bettelwurfhütte. Ignore this as it is the descent path. When you reach the wooded area, there are several yellow signs set back 30 metres from the road, one of which indicates 'Absamer Klettersteig' to the right. Cross the river and walk upwards along a vague scree path towards the rock face on your right-hand side. There are red and white paint markers on the rocks to signal the path. After 20mins you will enter a forested area, follow the small path for 5mins to reach the start of the klettersteig.

Day 1

The via ferrata begins with easy and enjoyable scrambling, quickly leading to a short steeper section. You then traverse in left to reach a deep gash in the cliff with a spectacular huge jammed block. Cross this block and make a rising traverse left with easy scrambling, followed by a short down-climb around 40mins in. The traverse includes a couple of short steeper sections and after another 25mins you will reach a distinctive deep cut gully with a white streak. Traverse the white streak to arrive at an exposed and impressive cable bridge which crosses the gully. This section is particularly dangerous for rockfall and you are advised not to hang around.

After crossing the bridge, begin another rising traverse left which becomes a little steeper and more sustained to reach a fantastic feature with two more impressive stuck blocks. This is a great spot for lunch! Traverse round both of these blocks before continuing upwards.

From the blocks, follow the route directly upwards via low-angled, easy scrambling and a gentle traverse leftwards for around 45mins until you reach a large open ridge on a grassy col. Follow the red and white paint markers along the ridge, mostly walking with very occasional sections of easy via ferrata, for another hour to reach the **Bettelwurfhütte**.

Built at the end of the 19th century, Bettelwurfhütte (tel 05223 53353, www.bettelwurfhuette.at, 32 bunk beds, 30 mattresses on the floor, open early June to mid October) offers incredible views across Hall in Tirol and Innsbruck and is popular with both hikers and ski tourers.

Descent

If you are not continuing on to complete the Westgrat and Eisengattergrat via ferrata, the descent from the hut to the car park takes around 2hrs 30mins. From the front terrace of the hut, follow the clear path due east which winds downwards for 2hrs to emerge onto the approach road next to a **water treatment building**. From here follow the road back down to the car park (around 20mins).

Day 2 (optional)

This loop is an excellent add-on to the Absamer klettersteig. It is more of a protected mountaineering route than a klettersteig, including some fantastic climbing moves, and takes you to the very summit of the Großer Bettelwurf with a stunning panorama across the Inn Valley.

There is a large wooden cross and a bench on the hillside directly behind the hut, from which a vague path leads steeply upwards. Take this path as it meanders straight up the hillside, very well marked with red and white paint markers. After 45mins you will reach a rocky gully where the fixed cables begin.

The route is clearly signposted with paint markers all the way and traverses rightwards, following sporadic sections of cable, involving mostly scrambling over often quite loose scree in the direction of the col that separates the Kleiner and Großer Bettelwurf summits. There are a couple of very brief, yet unprotected climbing moves which require reasonable confidence moving on low-angled,

Traversing the scree slope under the Kleiner Bettelwurf

loose and sometimes fairly exposed terrain. After 40mins, the path splits, 100 metres from the col and at the same height as it. Going left allows you to make a 20min detour to tag the summit of the **Kleiner Bettelwurf**, before returning back to the split in the path. Continue straight on and after another 5mins you will reach the col, with the Großer Bettelwurf's impressive north east face towering above it. From here to the summit is mostly steady and enjoyable scrambling, with a couple of exposed and loose sections. The final summit ridge can be snowy, but it is generally an exposed yet easy walk passing a large, triangular, rock-filled structure to reach the beautiful summit of **Großer Bettelwurf**, adorned with a huge cross and with views deserving of the effort it took to get there.

Descent
Reverse the last 50 metres of the ridge, past the triangular structure, and you will see cables dropping off down to the left. From here, descend steeply via a combination of scrambling and protected down-climbing, following red and white paint markers. Much of the descent is not hugely enjoyable, with a lot of the rock being loose and the route steep, but after an hour you reach a more civilised walking path leading back in the direction of the Bettelwurfhütte.

Just before you cross a large scree gully, there is a cut-out path leftwards, leading directly downhill to join the descent path from the hut. Take this direct route down, and allow 4hrs for the total descent from the summit to the car park in **Absam**.

Approaching the summit of the Großer Bettelwurf

Alternatively you can continue heading right, back to Bettelwurfhütte. The hut is only a 20min walk from this cut-out path so not a huge diversion it you need to pick up kit you left there, or a welcome relief if you simply want a pitstop before tackling the final part of the descent! From the hut, see the descent for day 1 which describes the route back to the carpark in **Absam**.

Starting the ascent from Matrei am Brenner, with the impressive Serles mountain looming above (Route 43)

Mountain biking is arguably the most popular summer sport in Innsbruck, as for many it takes the place of skiing once the snow has melted. Indeed, there are new state-of-the-art downhill mountain bike trails and bike parks popping up each year all over the mountains surrounding Innsbruck. The main ones are located at Nordkette and Arzler Alm on the north side of the city, and at Axamer Lizum, Götzens and Mutters on the south side.

There are also thousands of kilometres of designated mountain bike tours criss-crossing their way through the mountains, indeed over 5500km of trails can be found across the whole of Tirol. With regards to difficulty, the region boasts superb mountain biking terrain, having something for everyone from beginners to experts. Tirol is very proud to hold the title of having the longest mountain bike trail in the Alps in the form of the 'Bike Trail Tirol'. This impressive 1000km-long circuit loops around Tirol, is divided into 32 stages and in its entirety includes a staggering 27,000m of elevation!

Mountain bike rental is available all over the city, so it is not essential to bring your bike on holiday with you. Another interesting option, which is becoming increasingly more popular, is the rental of e-bikes. Specialist mountain e-bikes are electronically powered machines which have an integrated motor and are designed to tackle those undulating mountain tracks. As well as giving an enormous mechanical boost on those hills, they can also be propelled by pedalling; the faster you pedal the more help the bike will give you, so it is not all cheating! Designated biking maps are available from the tourist office, with a selection of mountain bike routes of varying difficulty. The possibilities

A spot of orientation looking across at the Nordkette chain (Route 41)

of mountain biking around Innsbruck are literally endless. Included here are six thoroughly enjoyable routes, from short rides up to mountain huts to a breathtaking full day tour through the Karwendel national park, and of course not forgetting Innsbruck's most famous downhill track, the Nordkette singletrail.

The mountain biking (and the road cycling) routes in this book are graded as either easy, medium, difficult or expert, taking into account the distance, total ascent and terrain. The timings are given as a rough round trip estimate and can vary considerably depending on the rider so should be taken as a guideline only.

ROUTE 39

Nordkette singletrail

Start	Mid-station (Seegrube) of the Hungerburg lift
Finish	Hungerburg
Distance	4.2km
Descent	1030m
Grade	Expert
Time	30–50mins
Terrain	Maintained mountain bike trail
Maps	Kompass Map 36 Innsbruck Brenner or Map 036 Innsbruck und Umgebung
Public transport	Public bus from Innsbruck centre to the Hungerburg cable car station or the funicular railway from Innsbruck Congress station to Hungerburg station, then from Hungerburg take the cable car up to Seegrube.
Access and parking	It is possible to drive directly up to Hungerburg and park there, then from Hungerburg take the cable car up to Seegrube.
Note	On Friday evenings the Nordkette cable car has longer opening hours, allowing riders to take their bikes up to Seegrube until 8pm.

The Nordkette singletrail is a true Innsbruck classic and an experience not to be missed for accomplished and expert mountain bikers seeking adrenaline and thrills during their visit to Innsbruck. Dubbed as one of Europe's most challenging and demanding downhill trails, it is a unique experience. The location of the trail, in the heart of the mountains high above Innsbruck, is truly spectacular, giving riders the exhilarating feeling of plunging directly down into the city as they twist and turn their way down the steep trails. Professional downhill competitions are held here regularly and the expert riders can complete the course in just 10 minutes!

Exit the **Seegrube cable car station** to the right, passing the access to the higher cable car and away from the restaurant. From outside you have a spectacular view

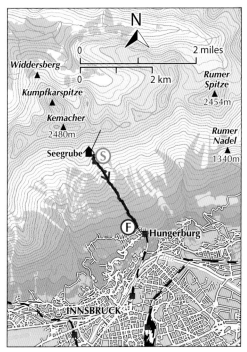

up to the mountains above, the winter playground for the expert skiers of Innsbruck. Here you will find a sign indicating the start of the trail, bending round to the right initially along a 4x4 track.

Around the first corner you will soon join the narrow mountain bike trail, which is very well signposted throughout, with clear signs at every junction making sure you are still on track. Be mindful of hikers, as the route occasionally crosses the very popular hiking trail, and although the signs make it very clear that it is mountain bikers

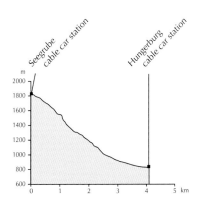

Clear signposting throughout

only, it is not out of the question that the occasional hiker may accidentally stray off the beaten path.

The trail finishes at the **Hungerburg cable car station**, from where you can either ride the funicular back down to Innsbruck, return to your car or cycle back to Innsbruck on the road. Alternatively, you could take the cable car back up and do it all again!

ROUTE 40

Karwendel loop

Start/Finish	Scharnitz
Distance	70km
Ascent	1600m
Grade	Difficult
Time	7–8hrs
Terrain	Well-maintained jeep tracks
Maps	Kompass Map 26 Karwendelgebirge
Public transport	Scharnitz can be easily reached via a direct train from Innsbruck, with the parking area at the start of the ride only a 7min cycle from the train station. From the station head out onto the main road through Scharnitz, turn left and cycle 400 metres to reach a cream-coloured church on the left. Turn left here and follow the directions below to the start of the route.
Access and parking	Pass through the village of Seefeld to arrive in Scharnitz. Turn right directly after the large cream-coloured church on the right-hand side of the road, signposted 'Karwendeltaler', and pass a grassy parking area on your left where the road splits. Take the right-hand fork following Hinterautalstrasse and after 450 metres cross a bridge and reach the parking area (pay and display) on the right-hand side. (If this area is full you can also use the large grassy area just 100 metres back down the road.)

This superb scenic day tour gently weaves its way through the Karwendel mountains, mostly along well-maintained, undulating 4x4 tracks, making for a delightful, sociable ride. The final section up to the Karwendelhaus is a bit of a slog but most certainly worth it. The second half of the tour after Hinterriss involves two 300m climbs, but the exhilarating descents which follow make them more than worthwhile. This is a little-known, little-visited area of the Alps and throughout the tour you are unlikely to meet more than a handful of people. The Karwendelhaus Lodge is a beautiful mountain hut and sits in a lofty position overlooking a spectacular valley. The views from start to finish are wondrous, the solitude second to none. This is a fantastic full day out and will fully warrant a big feed back in Innsbruck in the evening!

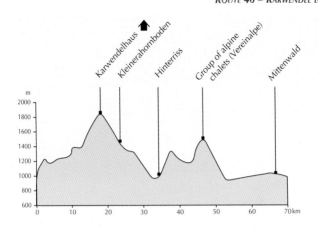

The Karwendeltal and Karwendelhaus are marked on the large wooden signpost next to the parking area. Follow the track as directed and 50 metres later the road branches off right, again signposted for the Karwendeltal and Karwendelhaus. Take this right-hand road and from there simply follow a well-established 4x4 track all the way to the **Karwendelhaus**, ignoring any subsidiary roads. The first 14km is a thoroughly enjoyable, gentle track, mostly flat with a few undulations, and the final 4km is a bit of an uphill grind.

> The Karwendelhaus (tel 0720 983554, **www.karwendelhaus.com**, 52 bunk beds, 141 mattresses on the floor, open early June to mid October) is well worth a long pit stop. Over 100 years old, it is a very impressive hut overlooking a secluded valley with an old-fashioned wooden interior and hearty, inexpensive food. No surprise then that it is popular with day trippers either hiking or mountain biking.

From here a short climb follows to **Hochalmsattel**, and then take a further 4x4 track downhill on a much more gravelly track and not as well established as the previous one but great fun on a mountain bike.

You will emerge at **Kleinerahornboden**, a four-way junction with two lovely wooden chalets. From here you take the right-hand path, following signs for Hinterriss and Falkenhütte, down to the bottom of the valley. After a long, fun descent you will cross a small bridge at roughly 1050m where the hiking trail branches off to the left, towards Hinterriss, but the bike trail continues straight

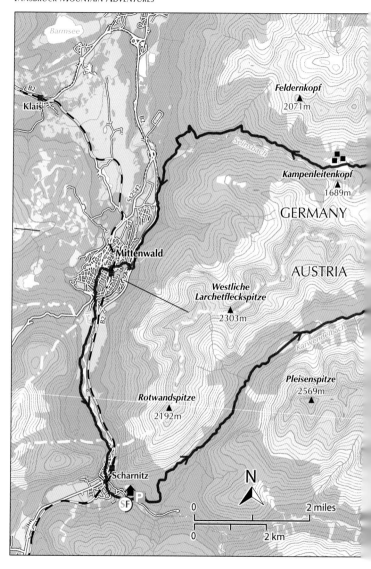

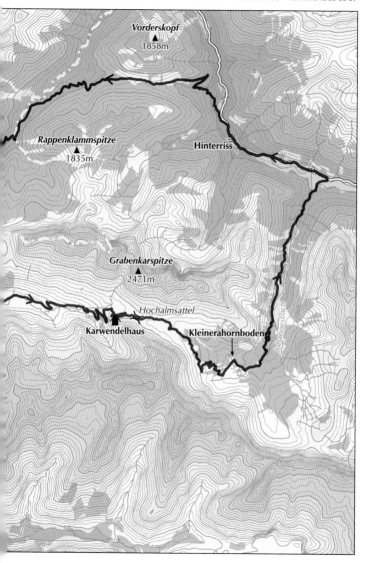

Enjoying the first major descent

ahead, signposted 'Hinterriss Eng', re-ascending and negotiating a few hairpin bends, before descending to arrive in the village of **Hinterriss**. Here there is a lovely little guesthouse and restaurant (Gasthof Zur Post), which is another great pitstop to recharge.

Gasthof Zur Post (tel 05245 206, **www.post-hinterriss.info**, open year round) serves hot food all day.

Follow the road north out of the village and 500 metres after the guesthouse, just before the road crosses the river, a small track leads off to the left, signposted for Vordersbachau, Ferreinalm and Vorderiss.

An initial 300m climb, following signs for Vereinalpe, leads to a thoroughly enjoyable and very welcome descent. This eventually brings you out parallel to the river that, despite the lack of a bridge, you need to cross! The water is shallow, so you can either brave it barefoot or try your luck crossing the rocks. The trail continues directly opposite on the far side of the river, with a mountain bike signpost, and follows a final 260m climb up to a delightful group of charming **alpine chalets**.

From the chalets, take the lovely long, smooth 4x4 track downhill direction Mittenwald. After 10mins make sure you take the easy-to-miss left-hand turn signposted 'Mittenwald' at around 1300m. After a further 20mins downhill you will emerge onto a main road near an army base. Follow the cycle path parallel to the road, clearly signposted as a cycle path, all the way to **Mittenwald**. After 1.5km you cross the river and continue on the cycle path parallel to the river, always following the cycle track sign. Eventually the cycle path runs out at the southern end of Mittenwald, and from here you join the main road back to **Scharnitz**.

 # ROUTE 41

Rinn to Rinner Alm

Start/Finish	Rinn
Distance	7.4km
Ascent	460m
Grade	Moderate
Time	2hrs
Terrain	Well-maintained 4x4 tracks
Maps	Kompass Map 36 Innsbruck Brenner or Map 036 Innsbruck und Umgebung
Public transport	Rinn is easily accessed via public bus direct from Innsbruck train station in just under 30mins.
Access and parking	From the centre of Rinn turn right directly opposite the ornate church on the left. Turn left after 100 metres, following two consecutive large blue parking signs and signs for Rinner Alm. The pay and display parking is on two tiers with ample space for cars.

Starting from the quaint and picturesque village of Rinn, this is a medium difficulty trail on the southern side of the Inn Valley. One of the shorter routes described here, it is ideal for those looking for a scenic workout without spending a full day on the bike. The high point is the lovely Rinner Alm at 1377m. With outstanding views across Innsbruck and beyond, it is a perfect place to refresh and refuel before the descent.

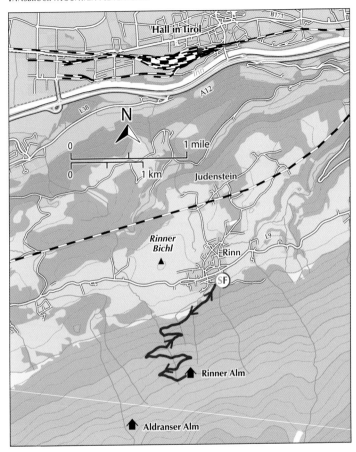

From the car park, retrace your steps back to the first parking sign and follow the small yellow hiking signpost pointing uphill for Rinner Alm. This very quickly turns into a 4x4 track and you will shortly reach a four-way junction. Bike trail number 518 for Rinner Alm is signposted to the right, with a sign showing information about the route. From here follow the 4x4 track for 3.7km as it winds gradually up through the forest to reach **Rinner Alm**. The final kilometre is slightly steeper but is well worth it for the views and hospitality at the top.

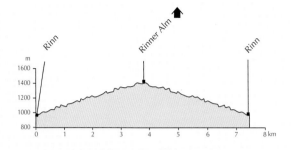

Serving arguably the best *kaspressknödel* around (!) Rinner Alm (tel 05223 78409, **www.rinner-alm.com**, open year round) is well known for its cuisine, and is a popular spot for hikers and mountain bikers, as well as having a great sledging track in the winter.

Descend the same way.

Enjoying the view from Rinner Alm

Heading down from the Rinner Alm

Extension

For those wishing to extend their day, this route can be easily combined with Route 42 (Aldranser Alm), by cycling down to the village of Aldrans and then following the directions to **Aldranser Alm** from there.

ROUTE 42

Aldrans to Aldranser Alm

Start/Finish	Aldrans
Distance	14km or 16km
Ascent	730m
Grade	Moderate
Time	2hrs 15mins
Terrain	Well-maintained 4x4 tracks
Maps	Kompass Map 36 Innsbruck Brenner or Map 036 Innsbruck und Umgebung
Public transport	Direct buses leave Innsbruck for Aldrans from the central train station, taking around 15mins. Make sure to double check the route as buses at certain times of the day will drop you directly outside the Aldrans MPREIS, but sometimes it is possible to stay on for a further two stops and get off at the hamlet of Fagslung, thereby avoiding the initial climb.
Access and parking	There are a number of on-street parking spaces in the village of Aldrans, or alternatively there is an underground car park signposted from the centre of the village.
Note	At just under 200m above Innsbruck, Aldrans can also be reached easily by bike.

This rewarding route is one of Tirol's marked mountain bike tours (554). It begins from the village of Aldrans which lies to the south of Innsbruck, 5km from the city centre and follows a well-established, easy-to-follow mountain bike trail which climbs steadily up to Aldranser Alm. The alm, set in a fantastic location with a sunny terrace and superb views, makes the 730m of height gain well worth it.

From the MPREIS supermarket in the centre of Aldrans, follow Bederlungerweg uphill, signposted for Tulfes and Rinn as well as Aldranser Alm. Follow this road for 1.7km until you reach a small roundabout. Here take the second exit,

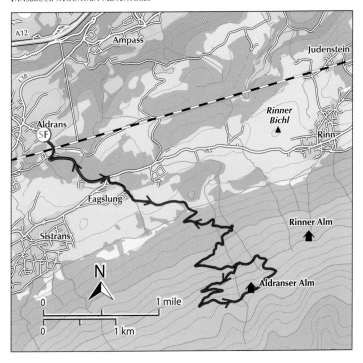

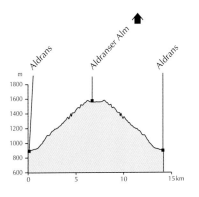

signposted 'Aldranser Alm', to pass through the tiny hamlet of **Fagslung**. The road quickly turns into a gravelly 4x4 track with fantastic views across the fields to the Nordkette mountain chain. Follow this 4x4 track as it climbs gradually uphill through a very peaceful forest until

A scenic descent from Aldranser Alm

you reach a fork in the road after around 3.5km. Here the choice is yours as both left and right lead to Aldranser Alm. To the left the final ascent is steeper and shorter, just 1.5km, whereas to the right the path is less steep but longer, at 3km. One option is to take one path up and the other down. Taking either route will bring you out at **Aldranser Alm** itself, in a lovely location perched on the mountainside with uninterrupted views across Innsbruck.

> Aldranser Alm (tel 0664 1516675, **www.aldranseralm.at**, open May until October, closed on Thursdays) offers traditional, hearty Tirolean food with fantastic views across the valley.

Descend by either path to rejoin the track back down to **Aldrans**.

Extension
For those wishing to extend their day, this route can be easily combined with Route 41 (Rinner Alm) by cycling down to the village of **Rinn** and then following the directions up to **Rinner Alm** from there.

ROUTE 43

Maria Waldrast tour

Start	Matrei am Brenner
Finish	Innsbruck centre
Distance	32km
Ascent	950m
Grade	Moderate
Time	4hrs
Terrain	Well-maintained 4x4 tracks with sections of narrow mountain bike trails
Maps	Kompass Map 36 Innsbruck Brenner or Map 036 Innsbruck und Umgebung
Public transport	As this route starts and finishes in different places, the only option is to take the highly enjoyable train ride from Innsbruck to Matrei to the start of the ride.

In the shadow of the impressive peak, Serles (2717m), this superb 32km mountain bike tour wends its way through beautiful alpine scenery. The high point is the stunning Maria Waldrast pilgrimage church, which at 1640m above sea level, is one of Europe's highest monasteries. The initial 700m climb up to the monastery can feel like a bit of a grind, but the gradient remains constant throughout, and the view, both during the climb and from the top, more than compensates for the effort.

Exit the train station in **Matrei am Brenner** and turn right on the main road. Follow the road for 700 metres through the very quaint village centre and turn left onto Mühlbachl to follow the sign for Maria Waldrast. Start climbing straight away, passing houses and farmland around several zigzags, until you reach the end of the main road, and a small tollbooth (bikes are free). Here a smaller track signals the real start of the route.

The road divides into a paved road for the cars, and a 4x4 gravel track for bikes and pedestrians. Continue up the track, which remains a steady gradient, always following the street lights which in winter light the way for the downhill sledging track. The impressive Serles Peak towers above you all the way, providing

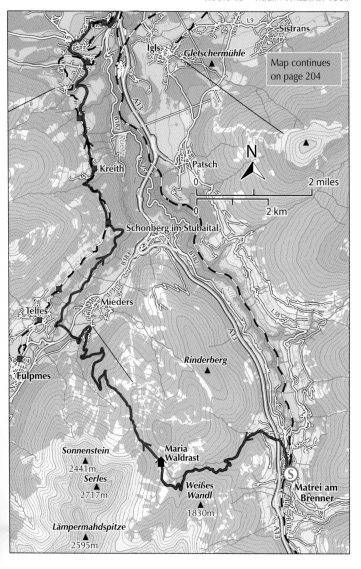

Sistrans

Igls

Gletschermühle

Map continues
on page 204

Patsch

N

2 miles

0

0

2 km

Kreith

Schonberg im Stubaital

Mieders

Rinderberg

Telfes

Fulpmes

Sonnenstein
2441m

Serles
2717m

Maria
Waldrast

*Weißes
Wandl*
1830m

S

Matrei am
Brenner

Lämpermahdspitze
2595m

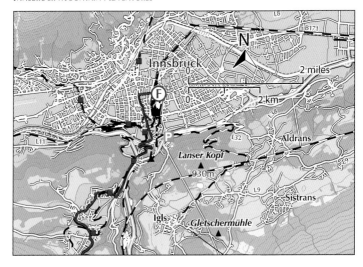

some excellent photo opportunities. After 7km of climbing you will reach a beautiful, open clearing, surrounded by mountains, and will see the **Maria Waldrast Monastery** up ahead of you, just a few minutes away.

Dating back to 1622, Maria Waldrast Monastery (tel 05273 6219, **www. mariawaldrast.at**, open throughout the summer) is well worth the effort to get to. Still a place of worship and pilgrimage, and a functioning monastery, it is a very hospitable place serving food and providing accommodation. Along with wonderful views of the Serles peak, this a great pit stop and it is understandably very popular with bikers and hikers.

Continue uphill from the monastery to quickly reach the high point of the ride. Immediately start to descend and after 5mins take the left-hand fork at the split in the path, signposted bike trail 'Kreuzweg 559'. Almost immediately after this, leave the main track to take the small path branching off to the right and continue following Kreuzweg 559. Here follows a short section of narrow and, in some places, fairly steep downhill biking, and at the next junction take the right-hand fork, signposted 'Mieders', to follow a 4x4 track which turns into a paved road and leads all the way to the village of **Mieders** itself. At the end of the road, with the cable car station on the right, turn left at the junction and follow the main road to a sweeping right turn, and immediately after this, swing right downhill,

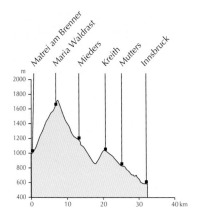

signposted for Innsbruck, Neustift and Fulpmes. Stay right to pass under the motorway then shortly afterwards cross the river and turn right at the other side.

Follow a beautiful winding road through lush, green countryside, initially downhill which then starts to steadily climb again and enters a forest. At the next junction, take the left-hand fork, signposted 'Kreith', to continue climbing up a forest path. This climb soon brings you out at the tram line, which you cross and

Starting the first descent from Maria Waldrast

turn right along a much more friendly gradient. Follow this path to re-cross the railway and enter the village of **Kreith**. Stay on the main road to leave Kreith and shortly reach Mutters. From here the most direct route back to Innsbruck is to simply follow the B182 all the way back to the city.

ROUTE 44

Mutters loop

Start/Finish	Mutters
Distance	19km
Ascent	880m
Grade	Moderate
Time	2hrs 30mins–3hrs
Terrain	4x4 tracks
Maps	Kompass Map 83 Stubaier Alpen
Public transport	The Stubaitalbahn tram (STB) leaves regularly from Innsbruck central train station and takes 30mins to reach Mutters.
Access and parking	Shortly after passing the church in the centre of Mutters, turn left onto Nockhofweg and follow this for 1km to reach the Muttereralmbahn cable car. Park here to begin the route.
Note	At just under 7km from Innsbruck, it is also possible to cycle to and from Mutters. A nice option is to take the tram to Mutters to start the route, as this is all uphill, then enjoy the easy downhill ride to Innsbruck on the way back.

This is a fairly challenging, yet thoroughly enjoyable, circular mountain bike route on the south side of the Inn Valley, passing no less than three excellent mountain huts along the way. The uphill is all covered in the first half of the ride and is a continuous gradient throughout, never getting too steep therefore allowing for a gentle ride up to the final hut, and an excellent downhill reward after lunch for the second half.

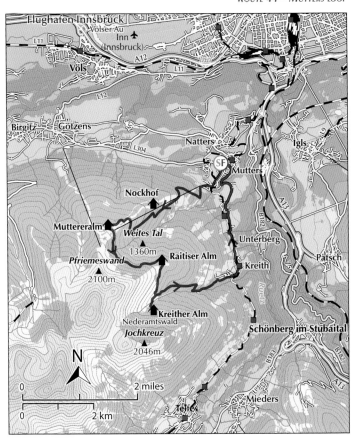

At the top of Mutteralmbahn car park you will see a series of signs indicating the route for the Bike Trail Tirol and the 'Muttereralmweg' trail number 510. Start the route along the latter trail following the direction of Muttereralm and Nockhof. From the car park the paved road quickly gives way to a gravel 4x4 track, follow this as it gradually climbs, winding up through the forest and repeatedly passing under the overhead cables of the gondola above. After 2km you will reach a right-hand turnoff for **Nockhof**, a lovely mountain farm which is great for a quick pit stop early on in the ride.

207

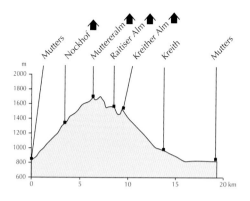

Nockhof farm (tel 0669 81371264, **www.nockhof.at**, open throughout the summer) has fine views.

Starting the descent from Kreither Alm

Continue upwards along the quiet gravel track at a similar gradient, and after a further 3km you will emerge at the top of the cable car and the **Muttereralm**.

More a mainstream restaurant than a mountain hut, Muttereralm (tel 0512 548330, **www.muttereralmpark.at**, open year round) is very popular and often busy due to its easy access at the top of the cable car. It offers superb views and traditional food.

There are numerous yellow trail marker signs on the walking path at the exit of the cable car station. Follow the signs left for Kreither Alm and Raitiser Alm along a lovely forest trail, passing a sign indicating that you are now on the Raitiseralmweg, bike trail number 512. A further 1km downhill will bring you out at the **Raitiser Alm**, which at the time of writing is permanently closed.

Continue along the trail around the alm to the right for another 1km to arrive at a junction from where you can see Kreither Alm nestled in the hillside opposite. Turn right here and after a couple of minutes of gentle uphill you will reach **Kreither Alm** itself.

A lovely traditional hut tucked away along a forest trail, Kreither Alm (tel 0677 61669613, **www.kreither-alm.at**, open early June until mid October) is very popular with mountain bikers and hikers enjoying a leisurely lunch or drink, the peace and quiet, friendly service and, of course, the superb views across the valley.

From Kreither Alm you reap the rewards of your uphill effort as from now on it is all downhill. Briefly retrace your steps back to the junction and this time follow the track signposted for Kreith. Some 3km of thoroughly enjoyable downhill riding will bring you out of the forest and into the small village of **Kreith**. Pass the tram stop and pass through the centre of the village, then stay on the main road to return to **Mutters** where you began.

🚴 ROAD CYCLING

Innsbruck and its environs are popular with cyclists of all abilities (Route 46)

Innsbruck is known as a 'Bike City' and it is likely that you will notice more than the average number of bikes on the streets. University students generally travel around by bike, and many other residents opt for bike over car to avoid the traffic. Bike hire is readily available and there are even bike points located around the city to explore on wheels, with the option to pick up and drop off wherever suits you.

Throughout Tirol the terrain for road cycling is varied, interesting and endlessly beautiful. Unlike many parts of the Alps, Tirol offers a lot more undulating terrain rather than having the choice of either relentless uphill slogs or long, long descents. The uphill exertions are very much available to those who seek them, but there are no end of less strenuous options, with the River Inn providing the perfect landscape for virtually flat, picturesque rides. Indeed, the Inn Cycle Path (Innradweg in German) is a classic 520km-long bike trail which starts in Switzerland, passes through Austria and finishes in southern Germany. It is one of Europe's longest and most charming cycle routes, and the 230km-long section through Tirol follows the River Inn along designated bike paths, keeping cyclists off the main roads for the majority of the ride. Many of the cycle routes

Dramatic mountain scenery on the descent from Mieming (Route 48)

around Innsbruck are off road, and many travel along quiet back roads, making Innsbruck an excellent place to give road cycling a go.

Cycling maps can be found at the tourist information office in Innsbruck, and of course there are a number of specialist cycling books available. Offered here are just a handful of the most enjoyable, mid-grade rides close to Innsbruck, from easy 20–30km rides up to a very scenic 80km loop ride.

The road cycling routes in this book (as with the mountain biking routes) are graded as either easy, moderate, difficult or expert, taking into account the distance, total ascent and terrain. The timings are given as a rough round trip estimate and can vary considerably depending on the rider so should be taken as a guideline only.

Important to note is that front and rear lights and a bell are legal requirements for a bike in Austria, and it is not uncommon for cyclists to be stopped and checked by police. You are often sharing your cycle path with pedestrians so the bell can come in very handy! Also be aware that motorists drive on the right in Austria, so take care when cycling, particularly on roundabouts.

ROUTE 45
Gnadenwald Plateau

Start/Finish	Hall in Tirol
Distance	30km
Ascent	350m
Grade	Moderate
Time	2hrs 15mins
Terrain	Asphalt roads
Maps	Kompass Map 36 Innsbruck Brenner or Map 036 Innsbruck und Umgebung
Public transport	Hall in Tirol is easily accessed by public bus from Innsbruck in just over 20mins, or by a regular train in less than 10mins.
Access and parking	From Innsbruck follow the A12 east for 4km. Take exit 68 signposted for Hall Mitte/Zentrum and at the roundabout take the second exit. Follow the river for 1km then turn left onto Bundesstraße and cross the river to arrive into the town of Hall in Tirol. Go straight over the first roundabout, following the road uphill, then at the second roundabout take the first exit to continue along Stadtgraben. As the road bends round to the right, pass straight over the next roundabout to find a small pay and display parking area immediately on the right-hand side.

This is a delightful circular road cycling loop starting and finishing in the lovely town of Hall in Tirol, just 9.5km from Innsbruck. With a round trip total of 30km and minimal height gain, this beautiful, scenic bike tour is accessible for all ages and abilities. All the height gain is in the first half of the ride, with the final 15km an enjoyable ride along the Inntalradweg – the river cycle track. Mid-way along the route is an option to take a detour up to one of Tirol's classic cycle routes: up to the Hinterhornalm, which is a further 6km in distance and 620m of height gain. While it is a worthwhile extension, it is more suited to experienced riders and should not be taken lightly as it adds considerable difficulty to the ride.

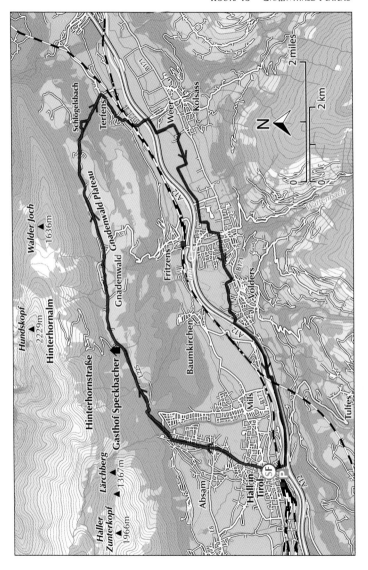

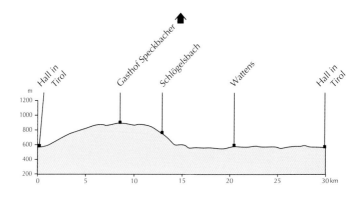

From the roundabout on the main road at the northern end of Hall in Tirol, follow the Salzbergstraße uphill in a northerly direction, crossing several roundabouts and always following signs for Gnadenwald. After 2.5km the road bends to the right, again signposted for Gnadenwald, and continues to climb gently uphill. A further 3.5km along a quiet and very scenic road will bring you to the **Gasthof Speckbacher** which is the high point of the cycle at 920m, and is also the point at which you have the option of taking the left-hand turning up the Hinterhornstraße towards the Hinterhornalm. This is a strenuous detour but those who make the effort will be well rewarded.

The route continues on along the **Gnadenwald Plateau** and past the quaint church of St Michael. After a further 2.5km be sure to take the left fork, in the direction of Terfens, rather than starting to head downhill. Passing through several small settlements, the road levels off and you will soon begin a long and winding descent, through the lovely hamlet of **Schlögelsbach**, to reach the village of Terfens.

At the bottom of the descent, at the road junction in **Terfens**, turn right, signposted for Neu Terfens and Weer. This marks the halfway point of the ride and all the height gain done! Continue on straight through the centre of Terfens to begin another short descent, first crossing the railway line, then the river, and then immediately after passing under the **motorway**, the Inntalradweg (Inn Valley cycle path) in the direction of Innsbruck is signposted on your right.

The final 15km of the ride follows the lovely, scenic Inntalradweg all the way back to the centre of Hall in Tirol, and is incredibly well signposted. There are a great number of turns and junctions along the cycle path, moving between rural and urban surroundings, so it is important to keep a close eye on the small

The quaint town of Hall in Tirol

signs for 'Inntalradweg Innsbruck', which are located at almost every junction, as some are easy to miss if you are not paying attention. The most notable junctions where there is potential for making a wrong turn are an easy-to-miss left turn upon reaching the industrial estate in Wattens, and then next when you reach the main road in Wattens. You will emerge directly opposite a Shell garage where you need to turn right then immediately left to continue in the direction of Innsbruck. You will soon see the church spire of Hall in Tirol and cross a wooden footbridge towards the town. Here, rather than continuing on towards Innsbruck, use the subway to pass under the railway line straight ahead, turn right on the other side and follow the road around to the left, which brings you back out on the outskirts of **Hall in Tirol**.

ROUTE 46
Innsbruck loop

Start/Finish	Marktplatz, Innsbruck city centre
Distance	23km
Ascent	180m
Grade	Easy
Time	1hr 30mins
Terrain	Asphalt roads
Maps	Kompass Map 36 Innsbruck Brenner or Map 036 Innsbruck und Umgebung
Access and parking	There are a number of paid parking options in and around Innsbruck centre.

An easy and picturesque circular loop, the route starts and finishes in Innsbruck centre passing through the quaint villages of Mühlau, Rum, Thaur and Hall in Tirol and returning along the delightful river cycle track. The minimal height gain is all in the first half of the ride, along a quiet road sitting high above Innsbruck and providing beautiful views of the city and across the valley.

From Marktplatz join the river cycle track heading east on the south side of the river and follow it for 1.7km until it runs out at the foot of the disused funicular railway line. Here turn right then immediately left to continue along the pavement and cross the river at the Mühlauer Brücke. On the other side of the bridge, cross at the traffic lights heading uphill until you reach a crossroads at the Gasthof Koreth in the village of **Mühlau**. Follow the road as it bends to the right and climb gently uphill to pass through **Arzl**. From here the road continues through lovely rolling fields with a great view across the valley.

Pass straight over the roundabout to reach the village of **Rum** and begin a thoroughly enjoyable descent down to the village of **Thaur**. As you enter Thaur, be sure to keep right at the fork, following signs for Absam and Hall in Tirol. Leave Thaur to begin another descent, with a fantastic view of the Karwendel mountains on your left. From here a gentle climb will bring you to the village of **Absam**, then a final short ascent to reach the outskirts of Hall in Tirol. Just after

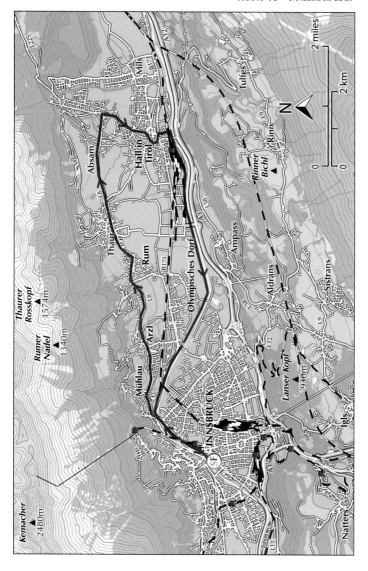

Kemacher
▲ 2480m

Thaurer
Rosskopf
▲ 1574m

Rumer
Nadel
▲ 1340m

N

2 miles

2 km

0

I25

A12

A12

Mils

Absam

Hall in
Tirol

Thaur

Rum

B171

I8

Olympisches Dorf

Mühlau

Arzl

I8

A13

Tulfes

Rinner
Bichl ▲

A13

Rinn

L9

Ampass

Aldrans

Sistrans

L32

L9

Lanser Kopf
▲ 930m

INNSBRUCK

SF

A12

A13

Igls

Natters

L11

217

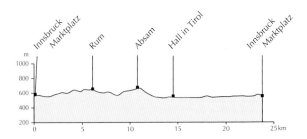

an MPREIS supermarket on the left, take the first exit at the roundabout heading downhill, signposted 'Hall i.T'. Cross straight over the next roundabout (third exit) to continue downhill and reach another roundabout signalling the town centre of **Hall in Tirol**. Take the first exit here to loop around the centre of the town, crossing straight over the next roundabout (third exit), which will bring you to a large road junction with traffic lights.

Turn left here and follow this main road for 200 metres before taking the right-hand bend opposite the old Gasthof Post (the name is written on the building), passing a yellow church building and a school (Volksschule). Keep left and after a further 200 metres turn right onto a road signposted 'Zum Innsteg'. Follow this road briefly before turning left down a small easy-to-miss path leading to an underpass beneath the **railway line**. Emerging out on the other side you will see a

Rolling farmers' fields with great views across the valley

218

sign for the cycle path west back towards Innsbruck, initially along a road running parallel to the train tracks.

Follow this road for 2km, and immediately before the road bends 90 degrees to the right, the cycle path is signposted to the left, where you cross the train tracks and join the path parallel to the river. The final 8km of the ride continues along this superb, picturesque cycle path, arriving back at the Mühlauer Brücke, where you re-cross the river and retrace the outward route to arrive back in **Innsbruck centre**.

 # ROUTE 47

Igls loop

Start/Finish	Igls village centre
Distance	30km
Ascent	680m
Grade	Moderate
Time	2hrs 30mins
Terrain	Asphalt roads and gravel trails
Maps	Kompass Map 36 Innsbruck Brenner or Map 036 Innsbruck und Umgebung
Public transport	If you are not in a hurry, by far the most scenic means of travelling to Igls is by using the number 6 tram line, known locally as the 'forest tram'. This travels over the plateau from the Bergisel tram stop in Innsbruck up to Igls. Alternatively a direct bus runs regularly between Innsbruck and Igls.
Access and parking	There are a number of on-street parking options in the centre of Igls or, alternatively, follow the road signs for the nearby Patscherkofelbahn where there is plenty of parking next to the cable car.

This is a beautiful and incredibly scenic road bike route through some of Innsbruck's finest countryside. Passing through several chocolate box villages on the southern side of the city, the views across to the Karwendel and the Nordkette mountain chain are truly spectacular, and the route interesting and varied. The very quaint village of Igls is well worth a visit in itself and provides a perfect spot for a pre-ride coffee and an after-ride lunch.

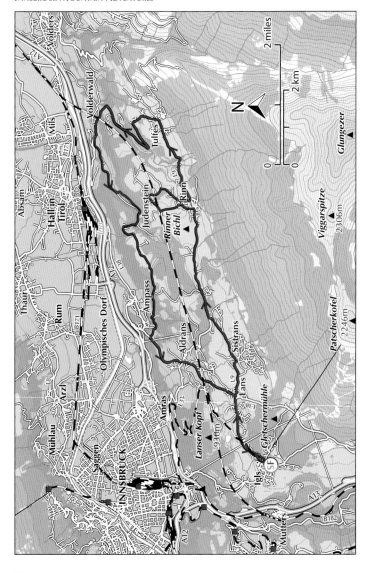

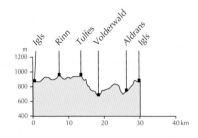

From the centre of Igls, take the Lanser Straße east out of the village, signposted for Lans and Aldrans, initially following the tram line on your left and passing the grassy parking area for the swimming lake, Lansersee. Continue along a gently undulating road to pass through **Lans** and go straight across at the four-way junction in the direction of Sistrans. The road starts to gradually climb, through rolling countryside and farmers' fields. Follow the main road through **Sistrans**, and after a further 1.5km, take the second exit at the roundabout, signposted 'Rinn 3km'.

Soon after entering **Rinn** you will see the beautiful baroque pilgrimage church on your left-hand side. Turn left just before the church, onto Kirchgasse, and shortly turn left again at the junction, following the sign for Judenstein to head along a beautiful, quiet road with uninterrupted views across to the Karwendel. Continue following the main road as it bears right through **Judenstein**, pass a campsite and another smaller church on the right, and take the next right directly after the church to start heading downhill towards Rinn and Tulfes. Turn right at the next small junction, then left shortly afterwards, signposted for Tulfes and Hall. Turn left here to rejoin the main road leading out of Rinn towards Tulfes.

Open roads and mountain views en route to Sistrans

Continue along the main road to reach **Tulfes** shortly after. Keep left to follow the main road towards A12 and Hall i.T. Enjoy the 4km-long winding descent from here down to the tiny village of **Volderwald**, although be sure not to miss the small left-hand turning just after leaving Volderwald, signposted for Ponyhof and Sturmhof, to start gently climbing again on a narrow road. The next 7.5km back to rejoin the main road are an absolute delight – a beautiful, quiet, undulating country lane surrounded by open green fields and mountain vistas. Up ahead you initially have a perfect view of the distinctive Patscherkofel summit. After 3.5km be sure to turn right at the T-junction, only signalled with hiking trail signposts.

After another descent, turn left at the main road to begin climbing up towards **Aldrans**. From the four-way junction at the village centre, turn left uphill to follow the signs for Lans, Sistrans and Igls. At the three-way junction in **Lans**, turn right signposted 'Igls' to retrace your initial route for 1.5km back to **Igls**.

ROUTE 48

*Innsbruck to the
Mieminger Plateau*

Start/Finish	Marktplatz, Innsbruck city centre
Distance	80km
Ascent	550m
Grade	Moderate
Time	5–5hrs 30mins
Terrain	Asphalt roads
Maps	Kompass Map 35 Imst – Telfs – Kühtai – Mieminger Kette or Map 36 Innsbruck Brenner
Access and parking	There are a number of paid parking options in and around Innsbruck centre.

High above the Inn Valley, the Mieminger Plateau not only provides wonderful views but is also one of the sunniest locations in the area. The majority of the route is relatively flat, with a long, enjoyable descent and a very gradual climb up to the plateau which makes it ideal for those looking for a long yet relatively easy road bike tour.

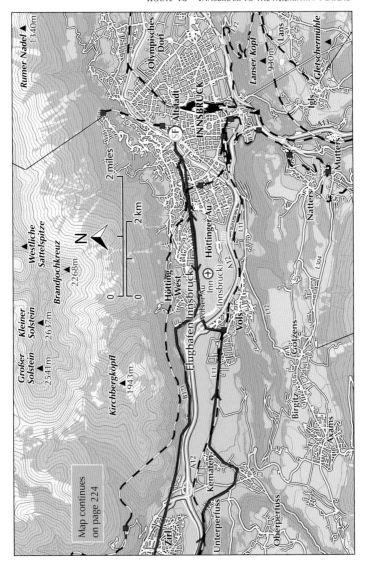

Map continues
on page 224

N

2 miles

2 km

223

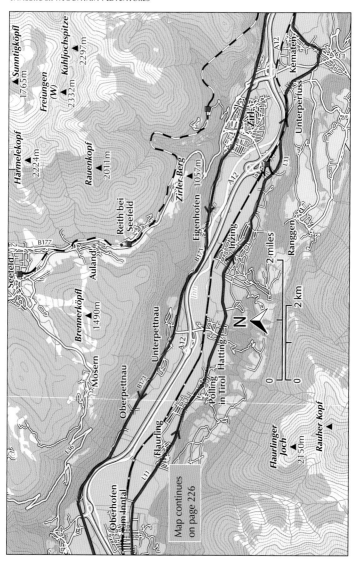

Map continues on page 226

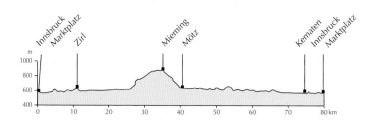

Starting from Marktplatz in the centre of Innsbruck, cross to the north side of the river and head west in the direction of Innsbruck airport. Follow the Kranebitter Allee which runs north of the **airport** and stay on the **B171** following signs for Zirl. Pass the Kranebitten campsite on your right and continue for 6km to reach the pretty town of Zirl. From the centre of **Zirl** continue on the B171 in the direction of Telfs for a further 8km to pass through **Eigenhofen**, **Unterpettnau** and **Oberpettnau**.

After leaving Oberpettnau continue along the B171 until you reach a roundabout, and cross straight over in the direction of Telfs. A further 3km will bring you to the fairly large town of **Telfs**, which, with a population of around 16,000, is the third largest municipality in Tirol. Ignore signs for Zentrum, instead follow in the direction of Mieming at the roundabout to skirt around the southern side of

High up on the Mieminger Plateau

225

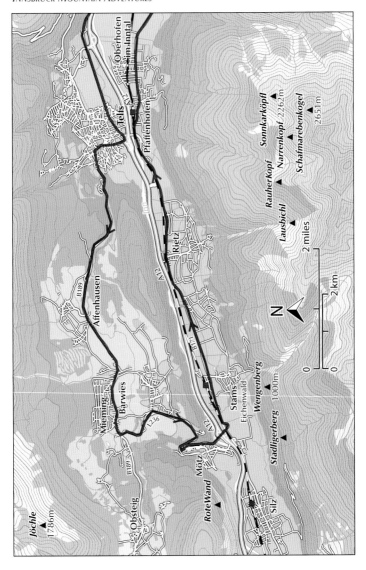

the town, and at the next roundabout follow the sign for A12 and Imst. Very soon after this sign bear right to follow 189 Mieming, then at the roundabout take the second exit, signposted for Mieming. Pass through a tunnel to reach a roundabout and continue in the direction of Reutte and Mieming.

Having left Telfs, stay on the **B189** to start climbing gradually up a picturesque road towards the plateau. After 4km you will reach **Affenhausen**, a quaint hamlet sitting on the Mieminger Plateau and surrounded by superb wide, open mountain views. From Affenhausen another short, gentle climb will bring you to the village of **Mieming** itself. Having passed through the village and just after the MPREIS supermarket on the left, take the last exit at the roundabout, signposted 'Mötz', to start heading downhill towards the Inn Valley. Here you can relax into a long, thoroughly enjoyable winding descent with beautiful views. Around 3.7km into the descent, turn right off the main road, signposted 'Mötz'.

Continue a short distance along this quiet road then turn left at the four-way junction following the sign for Innsbruck and Imst to pass through the village of **Mötz**. Cross the river and turn right signposted for Staudach and Bahnhof. Immediately after passing under the **motorway**, take a left-hand fork up towards the railway line then keep left to join a small track which runs parallel to the railway line. Follow this for 2km before turning right, following a small sign for Radweg, to pass under the railway line and at the roundabout take the third exit to join the **B171** in the direction of Innsbruck. There is a cycle path running parallel to the B171 enabling you to avoid the traffic.

After 7km on the B171 take the third exit at the roundabout towards Oberhoffen and Pfaffenhofen. From here follow this quiet, rural road which undulates gently along the valley back towards Innsbruck, passing through **Pfaffenhofen**, **Oberhofen**, **Flaurling**, **Polling**, **Hatting** and **Inzing**. From Inzing, a further 5km on the B171 will bring you to **Unterperfuss**. Shortly after leaving here cross straight over the roundabout following signs for Kematen. In the centre of **Kematen**, turn left at the T-junction, signposted for Völs.

Continue along the B171, crossing several roundabouts and always following the signs for Innsbruck and Flughafen (airport). Here you will find yourself once again on the Kranebitter Allee, north of the airport, from where you can retrace your steps back along the river and into the centre of **Innsbruck**.

ROUTE 49

Innsbruck – Telfs – Innsbruck

Start/Finish	Marktplatz, Innsbruck city centre
Distance	60km
Ascent	100m
Grade	Easy
Time	3hrs 30mins–4hrs
Terrain	Well-maintained cycle paths
Maps	Kompass Map 36 Innsbruck Brenner or Map 036 Innsbruck und Umgebung
Access and parking	There are a number of paid parking options in and around Innsbruck centre.

This virtually flat and very scenic cycle tour is a brilliant way of getting a 60km ride under your belt with very little effort. It follows the River Inn westwards, with mountains flanking the route on either side and very few roads to contend with. The simplest version of this tour is to follow the same route there and back along the river, however, the route described below gives a slightly alternative route, providing riders not only with a round trip, but also different terrain and an opportunity to pass through several picturesque villages giving more of a taste of life in Tirol. This route is suitable for riders of all abilities as there is no commitment; you always have the option to simply turn around and return rather than making it into a round trip, or to cycle out to Telfs, have a leisurely lunch and then take the train back to Innsbruck!

From Marktplatz head westwards along the cycle track on the south side of the river. It initially runs parallel to both the motorway and the river, but only for the first few kilometres. After 4km, you have the option of continuing straight ahead to follow the river (the simpler route – signposted for Landeck), however, the alternative, slightly more interesting route turns left here, under the motorway, signposted for Völs and Axams. Cycle towards the centre of **Völs** and turn right just before you reach the cream and yellow church on the left. At the end of this short road turn right onto the main road, passing the Völs Camping on the

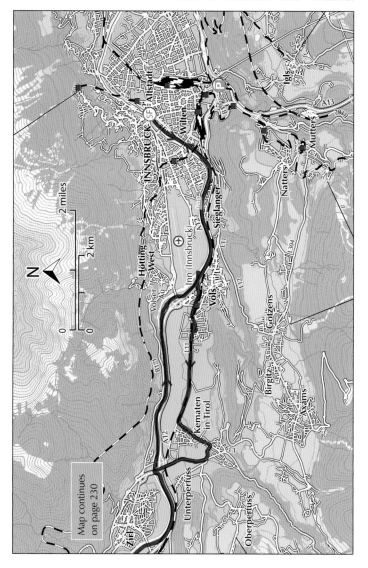

Map continues
on page 230

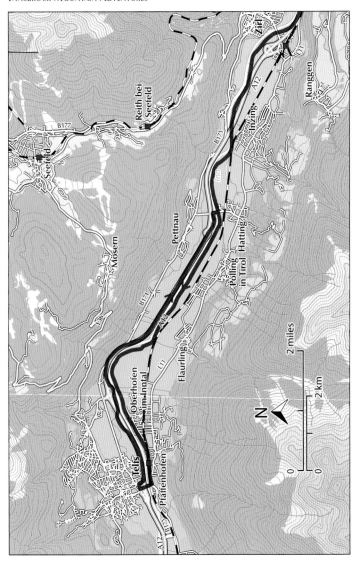

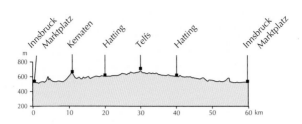

right-hand side. Upon reaching the next main road, turn left towards Kematen. At the roundabout on the outskirts of **Kematen**, take the first exit onto Melachweg and continue along this road, passing the Bäcker Ruetz bakery on your right (a superb lunch spot!). At the end of the road turn right onto the main road, passing under the **motorway** and heading towards the imposing Martinswand rock face which towers above Kematen. Immediately where the road bends 90 degrees to the right, turn left to join the cycle path along the river, and follow the sign in the direction of Landeck.

The next section is a lovely cycle path, following the river, but also passing through areas of forest, and with numerous opportunities to pop down to the river and take a quick dip should you so desire. Beware of uneven surfaces here where tree roots are pushing through the concrete. You will soon reach a road next to an MPREIS supermarket, cross here to rejoin the cycle path on the other side, always following the signs for Landeck. Having rejoined the path, you wind your way through farmland and open fields, surrounded by stunning mountains on every side. The track briefly turns into a gravelly 4x4 track for 1.5km to reach the small village of **Hatting**. Cross a road to continue along the cycle path, which now runs parallel to the railway line.

Follow this very scenic track for another 10km, still following the signs for Landeck, and shortly after passing through the village of **Oberhofen** you will reach a pedestrian bridge, signposted 'Telfs', which crosses the river to arrive in **Telfs**.

To return to Innsbruck, follow the river on the north side, signposted 'Innsbruck' at the bridge you crossed to arrive into Telfs. Continue along this lovely, picturesque cycle path, which runs parallel to the river and the motor-way, until you ascend a very short section to leave the river and join a main road crossing back over the river. Follow this road briefly and it will bring you into **Hatting** and back to the junction you crossed earlier. Turn left, following the sign for Innsbruck, to rejoin the path you came in on, and follow this until the section where you first joined the cycle path from **Kematen**. This time continue on along

Sharp lines en route to Telfs

the river, following 'Innsbruck', parallel to the motorway, to eventually rejoin the original route back to Marktplatz in **Innsbruck**.

⚙ CITY AND TRAIL RUNNING

Innsbruck has a strong relationship with running, and trail running in particular has become increasingly popular. Each April the city holds the Alpine Trail Running Festival, with races from 15km up to the 65km, and 85km ultra races. Another big trail run held annually is the Karwendel Berglauf 'vertical race'. This takes place just over the border in southern Germany, and with 1462m of ascent over just 11km, this is not a race to be taken lightly! As well as these big events, throughout the year there are also a number of other enjoyable runs held in the city, including the Innsbrucker night run, the Frühlingslauf (held at the start of April each year to herald the coming of spring) and the Silvesterlauf (the New Year's Eve fun run).

Across Innsbruck there are a number of locations which serve as starting points for running routes and which have a detailed map and descriptions of each route, as well as excellent signposts keeping you on track throughout. Between the city and the mountains, the terrain is varied and interesting and the routes can be anything from short distances of less than 2km up to tough 10–15km loops; perfect for runners of all abilities. These are all part of the 'Innsbruck In(n) Motion' network, a superb network of running routes

Heading through the forest on the Bergisel-Lauf (Route 51)

across the city and the surrounding areas (see www.run-walk-innsbruck. at for more details). Very few of the trails require car access, indeed many begin from the centre of Innsbruck, or from the top of either a funicular train or cable car. A selection of routes are listed here, ranging from short and easy to longer and more strenuous, and encompassing both city running and routes through the mountains and forests.

ROUTE 50

5 Brücken Runde

Start/Finish	Marktplatz, Innsbruck city centre
Distance	4.8km
Ascent	10m
Time	25–40mins
Terrain	Pedestrian paved river track
Maps	This straightforward route does not require a more detailed map
Access and parking	There are a number of parking options in Innsbruck centre, mostly pay and display or underground parking.
Note	The Inn promenade on both sides of the river is divided to provide pedestrians and cyclists with their own lanes. So as to avoid angering the local bikers, make sure that you are on the correct side of the path!

This virtually flat course following the river through the centre of Innsbruck passes or crosses five of its bridges along the lovely Inn promenade. At just under 5km this is a very accessible route, starting from the very centre of the city and suitable for all ages and abilities. Despite its central location, the pedestrian river track and abundance of greenery makes this route feel distinctly rural, and unlike many of the higher altitude trail runs it is also possible to run this route in winter. On a hot day the walls along the banks of the river will be lined with people enjoying the sunshine, making for a happy sight.

From the Marktplatz, join the cycle track heading east on the southern side of the river, and you will almost immediately come to a set of traffic lights over the Innbrücke, the main bridge in Innsbruck. Here you will see the first sign for '5 Brücken Runde'. Cross the road, keeping the river on your left, and continue to soon reach a picturesque pedestrian bridge, the Emile-Bèthouart-Steg. Cross the river here then turn left to now start heading west along the north side of the river.

Continue along with the river on your left, to pass under first the Innbrücke, then the Universitäts Brücke. This section of the run takes you through a lovely

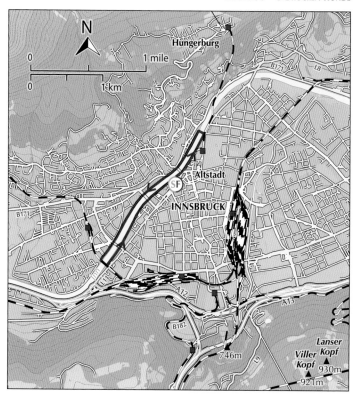

shaded park, past a children's play area and several small sports pitches. You will next pass under the Freiberger Brücke to continue following the river along the Arthur-Haidl-Promenade. Cross the river at the next bridge, the Karwendel-brücke, which is an impressive structure, combining a pedestrian walkway with the railway line above.

Turn left at the far side to rejoin the south bank of the river and to begin heading back east towards the centre of Innsbruck along the Franz-Gschnitzer-Promenade. You will soon pass back under the Freiberger Brücke with the university buildings on your right-hand side. After crossing back under the Universitäts Brücke, join the final stretch along the river to finish back at Marktplatz in the city centre.

The Emile-Béthouart-Steg near the start of the 5 Brücken Runde

 ROUTE 51

Bergisel-Lauf city run

Start/Finish	Bergisel car park
Distance	4km
Ascent	170m
Time	35–45mins
Terrain	Forest trails and paved roads
Maps	Kompass Map 36 Innsbruck Brenner or Map 036 Innsbruck und Umgebung
Public transport	The start of the route is a short walk from the Westbahnhof train station or, alternatively, tram number 1 runs from the city centre to the Bergisel ski jump. The car park is just a few minutes' walk from the tram stop.
Access and parking	Due to ongoing and extensive roadworks and bridge repair, the easiest place to begin this route is from the car park of the Tirol Panorama museum, which is also the official parking for the Bergisel ski jump. This is located on the southern side of the city, just a 25min walk from the city centre. There is also ample pay and display parking here.

This is a thoroughly enjoyable circular run starting from the outskirts of Innsbruck city and circumnavigating the impressive Bergisel ski jump. The majority of the route is through quiet, beautiful woodland next to the river and you will find it hard to believe you are just a mere stone's throw away from a bustling city. This is a rare find: a perfect combination of urban and nature running, and at only 4km long it is an ideal option for nipping out for a run in 'the great outdoors' without even having to leave the city.

From the back left-hand corner of the car park, take the small forest track leading downhill and bearing right. This path quickly passes under the **motorway** and enters a forest, taking you almost immediately away from the city. Keep bearing right and heading downhill to reach the river. Continue on the track to the right to keep following the river and you will shortly reach a **footbridge** crossing it. Turn right at the other side of the bridge to continue following the small signs for Bergisel-Lauf along a beautiful forest track which undulates gently alongside the river.

Continue along the river until the next **footbridge**, cross the river and turn right to start climbing up through the forest then across the motorway, until you emerge out onto the **main road**. Immediately before the road, turn almost 180

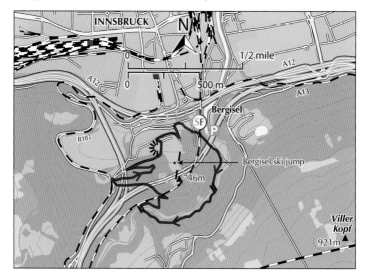

degrees to the right to take the narrow forest path leading upwards and away from the road, initially up some wooden steps. Now with the motorway down below on your right-hand side, you will soon pass a monument and a statue before reaching a wider forest road, where you turn left to start heading downhill. Just after passing a temporary barrier across the road, turn right at the junction past another barrier to continue downhill following signs for Bergisel-Lauf.

The final stage of this route takes you through a small residential area with fantastic views across Innsbruck. Turn right to start running parallel to the valley and to pass the entrance to the **Bergisel ski jump** itself. Continue downhill past a great panoramic **viewpoint** across the city and to the mountains beyond, following signs for Bergisel-Lauf at every turn, to soon find yourself back at the **Bergisel car park** where you started.

 ## ROUTE 52

Sill-Inn-Schleife

Start/Finish	Corner of Klostergasse and Sillufer, on the southern side of Innsbruck
Distance	10.9km
Ascent	55m
Time	1–1hr 15mins
Terrain	Pedestrian paved river track
Maps	Kompass Map 36 Innsbruck Brenner or Map 036 Innsbruck und Umgebung
Public transport	The start of the route is a short walk from the Westbahnhof train station, or, alternatively, tram number 1 runs from the city centre to the Bergisel ski jump. The starting point is just a few minutes' walk from the tram stop. See below.
Access and parking	The route begins on the southern outskirts of the city, in the direction of the Bergisel ski jump. From the Basilika Wilten follow Klostergasse around, past the tram stop and under the motorway bridge. There is a display panel under the pedestrian bridge which crosses the motorway, on the corner where Klostergasse meets Sillufer, showing the different running routes which start from this point. There is ample pay and display parking on Sillufer, right next to the start of the route.

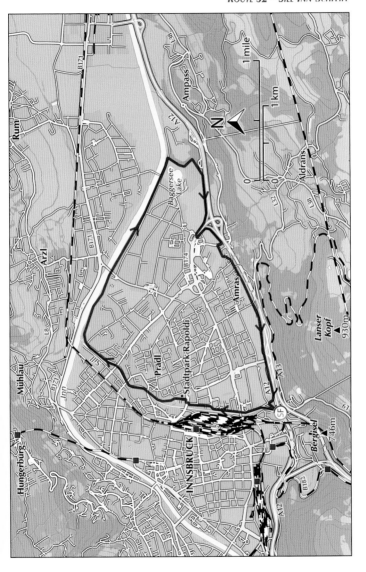

This is very picturesque, quiet and virtually flat circular route running along both of Innsbruck's rivers, the Sill and the Inn. The route takes in some of the lesser known parts of Innsbruck, passing through parks, fields and sleepy hamlets, along quiet stretches of both rivers, and reaching the Baggersee Lake, a very popular spot for swimming in the summer.

The arrows at the starting point for the Sill-Inn-Schleife are slightly confusing, seemingly pointing in the wrong direction, but rest assured the route begins by heading northwards on Sillufer, keeping the River Sill on your left-hand side. Continue following the river, and soon the road gives way to a short pedestrian section. At the 1km mark the road then bends to the right, away from the river. Turn left almost immediately after this bend, signalled by a small Sill-Inn-Schleife sign attached to a lamp post. At the traffic lights cross the road and the tram tracks, directly in front of the Städtisches Hallenbad (swimming pool) to see another small sign directing you to the right. Almost immediately after this, turn left onto a paved path, just before the **Stadtpark Rapoldi**. Cross a small wooden bridge to enter a park and continue along this footpath to rejoin the River Sill on your left, making sure to stick to the pedestrian path so as to avoid the wrath of any cyclists!

Shortly after the 3km sign, bear right where the River Sill meets the River Inn and follow this lovely path along the Inn for a further 3km until you reach the Deck 47 restaurant on the shores of **Baggersee Lake**. Just after the 6km marker you will see a sign directing you to turn right, crossing the road and skirting around the lake. Follow this quiet, pedestrian footpath until it runs out and reaches a road. Turn left to pass under the **motorway**, then immediately left again on the other side of the bridge (the sign is a little confusing here) to continue along another pedestrian path. Shortly after the 8km sign turn right to rejoin a road, then 50 metres further on take the first left onto a small, easy-to-miss track, which initially looks like a driveway. The gravelly footpath, called Shotterweg, runs along down to the right, with the prominent IKEA building over to the right.

Keep following the signs for the Sill-Inn-Schleife to pass through a small network of houses and reach another road. Cross straight over here to join Bichlweg and pass through another sleepy hamlet. Here the footpath crosses a grassy field to quickly rejoin a road. Follow this, running parallel with the motorway up on the left and past the Tivoli sports stadium on the right, for a further 1.5km, until the road bends 90 degrees round to the right. A final small sign will direct you left onto Wiesengasse, to find yourself back at the starting point.

⚡ ROUTE 53

Wolfele-Wilde-weg

Start/Finish	Hungerburg lift station
Distance	10.1km
Ascent	420m
Time	1hr 30mins–1hr 45mins
Terrain	Forest trails and 4x4 tracks
Maps	Kompass Map 36 Innsbruck Brenner or Map 036 Innsbruck und Umgebung
Public transport	Public bus from Innsbruck centre to the Hungerburg cable car station, or the funicular railway.
Access and parking	It is possible to drive directly up to Hungerburg and park at the lift station. From the car park walk along Hungerburgweg for 50 metres before turning right to join Gramartstrasse where you will see a large 'Innsbruck In(n) Motion' information board. This is where the run begins.

This thoroughly enjoyable trail run, easily accessed from Innsbruck without having to get into a car, is a medium difficulty run at just over 10km. The route begins from the top of the Hungerburg funicular railway, which runs from the centre of Innsbruck, and weaves its way along a network of forest paths on the north side of Innsbruck. Part of the 'Innsbruck In(n) Motion' network, the entire route is brilliantly signposted, ensuring that you are on the right track at every turn. The height gain is gradual and the scenery, views and atmosphere outstanding. It is difficult to imagine a more beautiful and accessible place to run while being only mere minutes from a city.

Follow the quiet tree-lined road for 1.5km, always following signs for the Wolfele-Wilde-weg, to pass the lovely **Gramarthof restaurant** on your left. Some 50 metres after the restaurant turn right just before the children's play area to head into the forest. Follow this forest trail which initially climbs briefly then crosses a small wooden bridge and flattens off around kilometre 2. You will shortly emerge out of the forest at a small **chapel** where you will see a sign

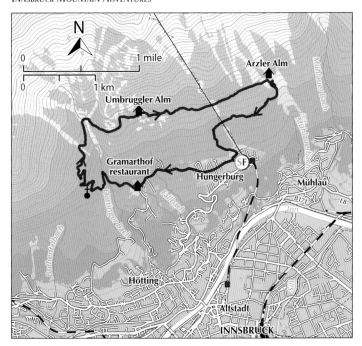

directing you uphill to continue the trail. Very soon after the 3km mark, turn right to continue up a slightly steeper hill. Follow this to a T-junction and turn right to continue along the trail which winds gradually uphill through the forest for 1.5km, eventually opening out to reveal beautiful views across Innsbruck and the Brenner Pass. At around the halfway point the path starts to descend briefly and then flattens off to reach **Umbruggler Alm**, a very impressive alpine hut, which opened in 2016.

Popular with both hikers and mountain bikers, Umbruggler Alm (tel 0664 3244543, **www.umbrueggleralm.at**, open year round) is a modern mountain restaurant tucked away in a large clearing. The views are spectacular and the alm is well worth a pit stop if you need a half-way break. It is one of Tirol's newest mountain huts, with a modern design and easily accessible from Innsbruck, and very popular with families as well as hikers and mountain bikers on a sunny day. It also has a playground for children.

Hikers on the Wolfele-Wilde-weg

From here take the path leading downwards away from the alm to start descending, and almost immediately look out for the easy-to-miss path which branches off to the left, signposted for Wolfele-Wilde-weg and Arzler Alm. Follow this narrow forest path until it is crossed by a slightly larger hiking path where there is no sign. Turn left here to shortly reach another marker sign which brings you out into a clearing directly underneath the cables of the Nordkette cable car. Watch out for mountain bikers here as you will be crossing several downhill trails. Take the lower path, which branches slightly to the right, signposted for Wolfele-Wilde-weg and follow the hiking trail through the forest, passing the 7km mark, to emerge at **Arzler Alm**, one of Innsbruck's most popular and most accessible huts.

Arzler Alm (tel 0664 6553395, **www.arzleralm.at**, open January until November) is a wonderful place for families with children, as there is a children's playground and a variety of animals to entertain them. Offering excellent service and traditional food, expect it to be extremely busy on a sunny weekend.

At Arzler Alm itself you will see a trail marker for the Wolfele-Wilde-weg, directing you downhill, through the children's play area and heading towards the valley. Descend a brief steep section directly below the alm and turn right onto a main path which then flattens out. Continue straight ahead on the undulating path, traversing the hillside to soon reach a four-way junction. Follow the sign here to turn right along a small path and continue following the Wolfele-Wilde-weg, then almost immediately look out for another easy-to-miss path branching off to the right, along a narrow and quite overgrown path. Stay high on this vague path, do not be tempted to drop down and join the main path, to shortly pass the 9km marker. Cross back under the overhead cables to continue straight ahead along a much more well-established path through the forest. Fairly soon take a left-hand path and wind your way downhill, bearing gradually right, to reach the main path. Turn left here to find yourself back at the **Hungerburg lift station**.

ROUTE 54

Mühlau Runde

Start/Finish	Marktplatz, Innsbruck city centre
Distance	9.5km
Ascent	280m
Time	1hr 15mins–1hr 45mins
Terrain	Mostly forest trails and 4x4 tracks with a few sections on paved roads
Maps	Kompass Map 36 Innsbruck Brenner or Map 036 Innsbruck und Umgebung
Access and parking	There are a number of parking options in Innsbruck centre, mostly pay and display or underground parking.

A huge amount of effort has gone into creating accessible and enjoyable running routes in Innsbruck, which are extremely well maintained and marked. This route is no exception: the Mühlau Runde is signposted at almost every possible junction, making the run very easy to follow. It starts at the Marktplatz in the city centre, passes the Alpenzoo and quickly becomes lovely, quiet and picturesque forest running, showcasing superbly the proximity of urban and rural.

From Marktplatz, join the river track eastwards, running with the river on your left-hand side. Shortly after the funicular railway station, cross the river via the wooden **footbridge**, signposted for Hans-Psenner-Steg and Alpenzoo, to arrive at a set of traffic lights. Cross here and take the uphill path directly opposite, clearly

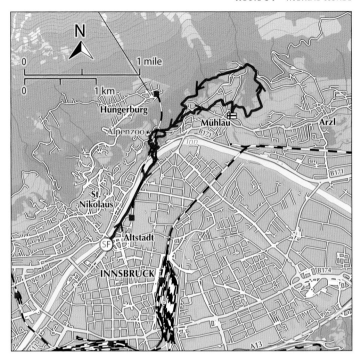

signposted 'Alpenzoo' and with a small sign for Mühlau Runde. The asphalt road winds its way up towards the Alpenzoo and quickly turns into a more gravelly 4x4 track. Follow this, ignoring any subsidiary roads, to reach a small, covered wooden footbridge. The Innsbruck **Alpenzoo** is above you, on the left-hand side. Cross the bridge, signposted 'Mühlau Runde', climbing gradually up a small track to arrive at a road. Follow the signs here for Mühlau Runde to turn briefly left onto Richardsweg, then almost immediately turn 180 degrees to join Schillerweg.

Very soon you will come to an easy-to-miss right-hand path, signposted 'Mühlau Runde' and leading downhill into the forest. Follow this path briefly downhill before re-climbing to join a road. Follow the trail marker to join Holzgasse and, after another brief downhill, take a left-hand turning onto Schlossfeld. Follow the well-positioned trail signs at every junction to pass through **Mühlau** and swing round past the pretty **cemetery** on your right-hand side as you gradually start to climb uphill.

245

Looking across Innsbruck to the Patscherkofel and Serles peaks from the grassy plateau on the Mühlau Runde

Having left the cemetery behind, the path then bears right at a small farmers' shack and very quickly enters beautiful rolling countryside, with superb views down to Innsbruck and across to the mountains beyond. Follow the 4x4 track to loop back left and head up a short but steep section of narrow path, which brings you out at a large grassy plateau, used to fly model aeroplanes; a handful of enthusiasts can regularly be found flying up here on good days. Cross this field to the far side to join a small track leading downhill, and a small rutted 4x4 track taking you back onto a paved road.

Once on the road, you will see a small sign on a lamp post directing you left for the Mühlau Runde. Follow this road downhill, bear left to cross the river onto Josef Schraffl Straße, and shortly afterwards stay right at the fork to join Schillerweg, also signposted 'Alpenzoo'. Follow this forest track for 1.5km until it meets a road, and you will find yourself next to the Alpenzoo funicular railway stop. Follow the path across the park, crossing under the funicular track, and above the wooden bridge you crossed earlier, climb briefly, skirting around the Alpenzoo itself, then head downhill along a lovely walking path, following the trail markers.

Follow this path winding downhill towards the river until you eventually reach a paved path which brings you back out at the traffic lights and the wooden **footbridge**. Retrace your steps from here to arrive back into the centre of **Innsbruck**.

🏵 FAMILY ACTIVITIES

A perfect spot for some quiet family time on the shore of Piburgersee (Route 60)

We all know how important it is for children to enjoy the benefits of the outdoors, and in Innsbruck and its surrounding villages there are several outdoor areas which have been put in place to cater for all the family. However, these are not outdoor play areas in the traditional sense; a great deal of thought and planning has gone into these wonderful places, managing to incorporate games and excitement into the outdoor learning experience. This way parents get to enjoy the great outdoors, and the children will have a fantastic day out without even realising they have been exercising!

Most of the activities described here involve interactive things for children to do or see throughout the walk, often in the form of challenges to tackle or puzzles to solve. Knowledge of German is not required to complete the activities as everything is shown by pictures. There are also some short family friendly walks, one up to an easy summit and another to a swimming lake.

ROUTE 55

Wusel lake trail, Achensee

Start	Maurach Prälatenhaus
Finish	Schwarzenau
Distance	3.8km
Time	1–1hr 30mins
Terrain	Easy tarmac path with very little difference in altitude
Maps	Kompass Map 027 Achensee
Public transport	It is possible to reach Maurach Prälatenhaus in just over an hour by taking a train from Innsbruck to Jenbach, followed by a bus from Jenbach to Maurach Mittelschule then changing buses for the short journey to Maurach Prälatenhaus.
Access and parking	From Innsbruck follow the A12 east for 34km then take the exit signposted for Wiesing/Achensee. Merge onto the B181 and at the roundabout take the second exit. Continue uphill for 11km and shortly after you see the prominent Kinderhotel on your right-hand side, turn left onto Seeuferstrasse. There is pay and display parking on the left. From the parking, follow the tarmac road for around 350 metres, and just after the Boat House (Boothaus) and a road barrier, you will see in front of you the large display board signalling the start of the Wusel Trail. Here children can collect their Wusel Trail cards ready for the adventure!
Activity	Pushchair-friendly walking or cycling trail with activity stations
Age range	From age 4

Around a 45min drive from Innsbruck, a trip to Lake Achensee is an absolute must. The lake itself is stunning, and there are endless possibilities for every kind of outdoor sport, from hiking and swimming, to mountain biking, climbing and windsurfing. The Wusel Lake Trail is a wonderful day out for the whole family. With play stations, puzzles to solve, climbing areas, challenges to complete, a sound station with instruments, sand pits and swimming bays positioned along the route, boredom and complaints are not likely to factor highly in your day.

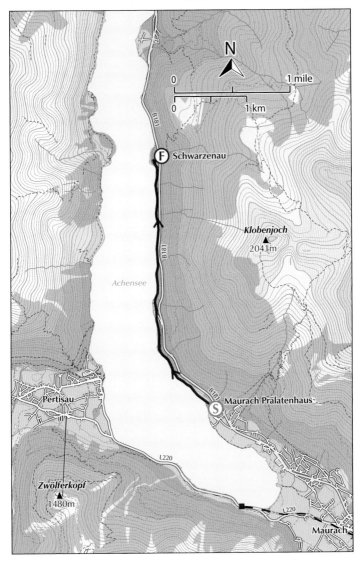

The sandy beach near the start of the first station on the Wusel trail

The Wusel lake trail starts out from **Maurach Prälatenhaus**, and follows a delightful path along the shore of the lake to Schwarzenau. There are 17 individual stations throughout the trail, all offering something fun for children to do. At the start they collect their 'Wusel card', which must be stamped with a letter at each station, and if they manage to get all the way to the end, and stamp all the fields in their Wusel card to reveal the mystery words, they either post their card in the box to receive a prize through the post, or hand it in at the **Camping Schwarzenau** to receive their prize there and then.

The path is completely pushchair friendly, and also very popular with cyclists, so the trail can also be completed by bike. You can either return the same way along the lake, or alternatively take a bus back from Schwarzenau to Prälatenhaus.

ROUTE 56

Ghost trail, Oberperfuss

Start	Top station (Stiglreith) of the Rangger-Köpfl gondola, Oberperfuss
Finish	Speichersee reservoir, Rangger-Köpfl
Distance	1.6km
Ascent	200m
Time	1hr 30mins
Terrain	Forest path
Maps	Kompass Map 36 Innsbruck Brenner or Map 036 Innsbruck und Umgebung
Public transport	Regular, direct buses run between Innsbruck and Oberperfuss.
Access and parking	From Innsbruck follow the A12 west for 8km to take exit 87 – Zirl-Ost. Keep right at the junction, follow this road for 2km and take the first exit at the roundabout. Then take the first left onto Oberperfer Landesstraße and after 300 metres turn left again to stay on Oberperfer Landesstraße. Follow this for just under 2km and turn right onto Peter-Anich-Weg. You will shortly see the lift station on the left-hand side where you can park.
Activity	Hiking trail with activity stations
Age range	From age 4

An ideal family day out, the Ghost trail in Oberperfuss is a 1.6km hiking trail which winds its way through the forest at the top of the Rangger-Köpfl gondola, finishing at the wonderfully picturesque Speichersee reservoir. Some 21 activity stations will keep children entertained, not least thanks to the 'Baumbarts': upside-down trees with exposed roots for hair and curious carved faces. Much to the delight of most children, pushing a button will even prompt these intriguing characters to speak (albeit in German!).

As with most outdoor activities in Innsbruck, there is no shortage of refreshment stops, with the **Stiglreith restaurant** located at the start of the route, and the **Sulzstich restaurant** awaiting you at the reservoir, with a kids' playground for those who still have some energy left.

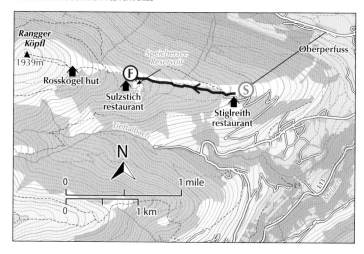

Stiglreith restaurant (tel 05232 77130, open daily during the summer) and
Sulzstich restaurant (tel 06644 111666, open weekends from mid June, then
daily from July) both serve home-cooked food and offer panoramic views
looking down the Inn Valley.

One of the many 'Baumbarts' who speak to you along the way

For ambitious families wishing to extend their day, the **Rosskogel hut**, a little higher up the mountain, is well worth the extra effort.

Rosskogel hut (tel 05232 81419, **www.rosskogelhuette.tirol**, open July until September) boasts wonderful views across the Inn Valley with excellent food and friendly staff.

Descend back down to Stiglreith the same way or walk the short distance up to the middle station and descend by cable car.

 ROUTE 57

Scheibenweg trail

Start/Finish	Mid-station (Froneben) of the Schlick 2000 ski area, Fulpmes
Distance	2km
Ascent	215m
Time	1hr 20mins (50mins up to the start of the trail, 30mins walking down)
Terrain	Easy hiking path
Maps	Kompass Map 36 Innsbruck Brenner or Map 036 Innsbruck und Umgebung
Public transport	Schlick can be easily reached by using the Stubaital scenic tram directly from the centre of Innsbruck.
Access and parking	Follow signs from the village centre of Fulpmes to reach the large parking area at the foot of the Schlick 2000 cable car.
Activity	Walking trail with activity stations
Age range	From age 4

Filled with excitement, challenges and speed, the Scheibenweg trail will not fail to inspire and delight even the most unwilling children with little or no interest in 'going for a hike'. Children will not even realise they are exercising as they challenge themselves and feel a sense of achievement trying their best to beat their wooden disk. The wide, easy path is also accessible for pushchairs, making the Scheibenweg trail an entirely family friendly day out.

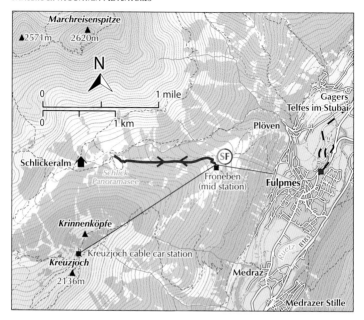

Children collect a wooden disk from the cash desk at the bottom of the cable car, which costs €1, plus a €2 deposit. There are wooden 'stations' throughout the trail, providing children with challenges and problems to solve, the first of which can be found at the Panoramasee Lake. The disk rolls down a wooden track and children must try to outrun it before moving on to the next station. Continue along the wooden disk track via the numerous stations along the route, back down to Froneben, the cable car mid-station.

The most rewarding option is to hike to the start of the trail from Froneben, the mid-station of the cable car, through a lovely shaded forest and up to the beautiful Schlick Panoramasee Lake. This takes just under an hour. Alternatively, to avoid uphill altogether, it is possible to start from the top station of the Kreuzjoch cable car and walk down to the lake via the Schlickeralm mountain hut.

ROUTE 58
Kugelwald Adventure World, Glungezer

Start/Finish	Top station of the Halsmarter lift, Glungezer, Tulfes
Terrain	Children's play area and forest
Maps	Kompass Map 36 Innsbruck Brenner or Map 036 Innsbruck und Umgebung
Public transport	A public bus runs regularly between Innsbruck and Tulfes.
Access and parking	From Innsbruck follow the A12 east for 4km then take exit 68 – Hall Mitte. At the roundabout, take the second exit onto B171a. Follow this for 7km to reach Tulfes. Once in the village turn left onto Glungezerstraße, then after 130 metres turn right, you will see the lift ahead of you and can park here. A 20min ride on the Glungezer two-man chairlift will bring you to the mid-station, just behind which is the Gasthof Halsmarter restaurant where you can collect the wooden balls for a small fee plus a deposit. You cannot miss the entrance to the Kugelwald, right next to the restaurant with a large wooden sign and information board.
Activity	Adventure playground with giant wooden marble-runs
Age range	From age 3

Kugelwald (literally meaning 'ball forest') on Glungezer proudly holds the title of the biggest wooden ball track in the world. It covers 7000 square metres with more than 200 metres of wooden tracks, all made by local carpenters with locally sourced materials. The adventure is all neatly contained, under shady trees with picnic benches, so adults can sit back and relax while the children roam free, chasing their wooden ball down the tracks, trying out all the different activities, stations and obstacles, challenging their minds as well as expending energy.

This wonderful place will keep children entertained all day and lunch is covered too: Gasthof Halsmarter not only has superb views but it also has an excellent playground.

Gasthof Halsmarter (tel 0650 9628536, **www.halsmarter.at**, open early June until early October) is an ideal lunch spot for all.

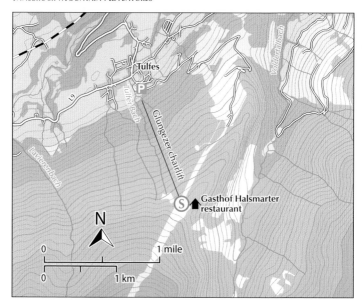

Fun for all ages

ROUTE 59

Patscherkofel summit path

Start/Finish	Top station of the Patscherkofel lift, Igls
Distance	5km
Ascent	300m
Time	1hr 40mins (1hr uphill, 40mins down)
Terrain	Easy, wide 4x4 track
Maps	Kompass Map 36 Innsbruck Brenner or Map 036 Innsbruck und Umgebung
Public transport	A regular bus runs between Innsbruck and Igls, or alternatively a slower yet incredibly scenic option is to take tram number 6, affectionately known by the locals as the 'forest tram', from the centre of Innsbruck up to Igls.
Access and parking	From Innsbruck follow Igler Straße until you reach the village of Igls. Turn left onto Hilberstraße and follow this for 500 metres to reach the Patscherkofel lift station where there is ample parking.
Activity	Pushchair-friendly walk
Age range	Suitable for all ages

The Patscherkofel cable car is located in Igls, south of Innsbruck, one of the Inn Valley's most quaint and picturesque villages and well worth a visit in itself. With its impressive needle pointing straight up into the sky, the Patscherkofel peak is undoubtedly the most distinctive summit point in the Innsbruck Valley, and can be seen from many miles away. It is not only a superb viewpoint, but it is also easily accessible via a wide footpath which is not steep and can be tackled with a pushchair.

From the top station of the cable car, walk up and behind the lift station where you will see the classic Zirbenweg hike heading off left, and signs for Gipfelstube up to the right. Follow the signs for the Gipfelstube to join the wide 4x4 track which winds gently uphill to reach the summit of **Patscherkofel** (2246m). The views across both the Inn Valley and Wipptal Valley are continuously superb, and this is a great way of reaching a prominent peak with minimal effort. To top it off there is also a lovely little mountain restaurant, **Restaurant Gipfelstube**, on the summit itself.

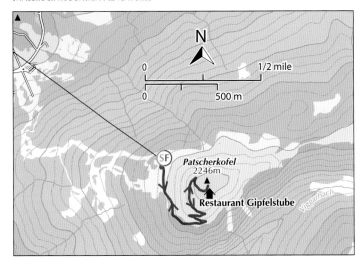

Restaurant Gipfelstube (tel 0664 9259351, **www.gipfelstube.at**, open year round) is a just reward for your efforts.

The summit path can also easily be linked with numerous other walks which begin at Patscherkofel, including the classic Zirbenweg walk (Route 2).

A great family hike, with very scenic rewards

ROUTE 60

Piburgersee

Start/Finish	Piburg
Maps	Kompass Map 35 Imst – Telfs – Kühtai – Mieminger Kette
Public transport	It is possible to reach Piburg from Innsbruck in just under an hour by taking a train from Innsbruck to Oetz, then from here a short bus journey will take you to Piburg.
Access and parking	From the centre of Oetz, turn right onto Piburger Straße. Follow this for 2km to reach a pay and display car park in the hamlet of Piburg. From the car park, follow the signs for Piburgersee, just a 500-metre walk to the lake itself. Alternatively the lake can be reached via a number of hiking trails from the nearby villages of Oetz, Sautens and Habichen.
Activity	Walking and cycling trails, lake swimming, fishing, boat rental
Age range	Suitable for all ages

An official area of outstanding natural beauty, the Piburgersee is a stunning, secluded, natural lake in the Ötztal Valley. Despite its elevation of 915m, Piburgersee is one of Tirol's warmest swimming lakes, reaching temperatures of up to 25°C during the summer months. Surrounded by impressive mountain vistas and boasting a number of gentle walking trails, there are plenty of activities for all the family to enjoy such as boat rental, swimming, mountain biking, including the Ötztal MTB Trail, as well as fishing, hiking and two lakeside restaurants. A lovely forest path circumnavigates the lake, taking less than an hour in total. With almost no altitude gain it is not a strenuous walk and sections are also suitable for pushchairs.

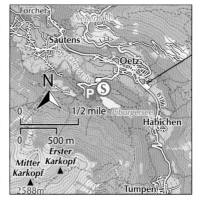

APPENDIX A
Route summary tables

All figures quoted are from start point to finish point.

Day walks

Route no	Route	Start/Finish	Distance	Ascent	Time	Page
1	Innsbrucker Almenweg	Mutterer Alm/Birgitzkopflhaus	5km	450m	2hrs 30mins	41
2	Zirbenweg	Top station of the Patscherkofel lift, Igls/ Top station of the Glungezer lift, Tulfes	7km	200m	2hrs 30mins	45
3	Grawa waterfall	Tschangelair Alm, Stubaital	5km	190m	1hr 30mins	48
4	Dreiseen hiking trail	Alpenrose Hotel, Kühtai	9.5km	350m	3hrs	51
5	Elferhütte	Top station of the Elferbahn gondola, Neustift	8.2km	700m	4hrs	54
6	Three lakes, Seefeld Plateau	Seefeld	12.3km	350m	4hrs	57
7	Arzler Alm	Hungerburg (funicular top station)	4km	210m	50mins	61
8	Aldranser Alm	Sistrans	10km	600m	3hrs	63
9	Bodenstein Alm	Hungerburg (funicular top station)	14km	800m	4hrs	66
10	Kreither Alm	Kreith	8km	490m	3hrs	70

Adventure walks and scrambles

Route no	Route	Start/Finish	Ascent	High point	Time	Grade	Page
11	Wildewasserweg	Grawa Alm	1060m	2540m	6hrs 30mins	N/a	75
12	Südlicher and Nordlicher Polleskogel	Ötztaler Gletscherstrasse	225m	3035m	2–3hrs	1–2	79
13	Glungezer klettersteig	Top station of the Glungezer lift, Tulfes	550m	2610m	3hrs 30mins	2	82
14	Brandjochspitze	Mid-station of the Hungerburg lift	690m (290m on the ridge)	2559m	6hrs 30mins	3	84
15	Nordgrat–Vordere Sommerwand	Oberissalm	900m (430m on the ridge)	2676m	7hrs	3	87
16	Nordgrat Zwölferkogel	Alpenrose Hotel, Kühtai	970m (380m on the ridge)	2988m	6hrs	3 (mostly 1 and 2)	90

Overnight hut trips

Route no	Route	Start/Finish	Distance	Ascent	Time	Number of days	Page
17	Halltal hike	Absam	11.2km or 18km	1510m	6hrs 30mins or 7hrs 30mins	2	95
18	Nordkette traverse	Top station of the Hungerburg lift/Absam	19.7km	770m (with 2050m descent)	9hrs	3	99
19	Karwendel traverse	Scharnitz/Stans	51km	2300m (with 2700m descent)	17hrs 30mins	3	105
20	Rofan Range hike	Kramsach/Erfurter Hütte, or Maurach	19km	2050m	9hrs 30mins or 11hrs	2	112

Alpine mountaineering routes

Route no	Route	Start/Finish	Ascent	High point	Time	Number of days	Grade	Page
21	Habicht	Neustift or Gschnitz/ Neustift	2310m, 1480m or 2040m	3277m	13½, 9½ or 11hrs	2	PD	119
22	Wilder Freiger	Grawa Alm	1900m	3418m	13hrs 30mins	2	F+	125
23	Zuckerhütl	Schaufeljoch Col station on the Stubai lift	620m	3507m	8–10hrs	2	PD+	130
24	Wildspitze	Vent	1860m or 1400m	3772m	9½–12hrs	2	F+/PD	134

Sport climbing

Route	Area	Grade	Page
25	Arzbergklamm	3–7a+	140
26	OeAV klettergarten	3–7b	142
27	Engelswand	3–8a+	144
28	Rofan cragging, Achensee	3–6b	146
29	Klettergarten Oetz	3–7c	149
30	Emmentaler multi-pitch	5a	151

Via ferratas

Route no	Route	Start/Finish	Time	Grade	Page
31	Innsbrucker klettersteig	Top station of the Hungerburg lift/Mid-station of the Hungerburg lift	4-5 or 6–8hrs 30mins	C	155
32	Achensee 5 Gipfel	Top station of the Rofan seilbahn, Maurach	6hrs 15mins	D	159
33	Crazy Eddy klettersteig	Silz	2hrs 20mins	C or D	163
34	Peter Kofler klettersteig	Sankt Jodok	2hrs 50mins	C	166
35	Ochsenwand/Schlicker klettersteig	Top station of the Schlick 2000 ski area, Fulpmes/Mid-station of the Schlick 2000 ski area	7hrs	C/D	169
36	Geierwand klettersteig	Haiming	3hrs 45mins	C	173
37	Kühtai Panorama klettersteig	Top station of the Dreiseenbahn lift, Kühtai/Alpenrose Hotel, Kühtai	4hrs	D/E	176
38	Absamer klettersteig	Absam	7hrs 45mins, or 11hrs 30mins–12hrs (over 2 days)	C	179

Mountain biking

Route no	Route	Start/Finish	Distance	Ascent	Time	Grade	Page
39	Nordkette singletrail	Mid-station of the Hungerburg lift/Hungerburg	4.2km	(1030m descent)	30–50mins	Expert	187
40	Karwendel loop	Scharnitz	70km	1600m	7–8hrs	Difficult	190
41	Rinn to Rinner Alm	Rinn	7.4km	460m	2hrs	Moderate	195

Route no	Route		Start/Finish	Distance	Ascent	Time	Grade	Page
42	Aldrans to Aldranser Alm	Aldrans		14km or 16km	730m	2hrs 15mins	Moderate	199
43	Maria Waldrast tour	Matrei am Brenner/Innsbruck centre		32km	950m	4hrs	Moderate	202
44	Mutters loop	Mutters		19km	880m	2hrs 30mins –3hrs	Moderate	206

Road cycling

Route no	Route	Start/Finish	Distance	Ascent	Time	Grade	Page
45	Gnadenwald Plateau	Hall in Tirol	30km	350m	2hrs 30mins	Moderate	212
46	Innsbruck loop	Marktplatz, Innsbruck city centre	23km	180m	1hr 30mins	Easy	216
47	Igls loop	Igls village centre	30km	680m	2hrs 30mins	Moderate	219
48	Innsbruck to the Mieminger Plateau	Marktplatz, Innsbruck city centre	80km	550m	5–5hrs 30mins	Moderate	222
49	Innsbruck – Telfs – Innsbruck	Marktplatz, Innsbruck city centre	60km	100m	3.5–4hrs	Easy	228

City and trail running

Route no	Route	Start/Finish	Distance	Ascent	Time	Page
50	5 Brücken Runde	Marktplatz, Innsbruck city centre	4.8km	10m	25–40mins	234
51	Bergisel-Lauf city run	Bergisel carpark	4km	170m	35mins–45mins	236

52	Sill-Inn-Schleife	Southern side of Innsbruck	10.9km		55m	1–1hr 15mins	238
53	Wölfele-Wilde-weg	Hungerburg lift station	10.1km		420m	1hr 30mins–1hr 45mins	241
54	Mühlau Runde	Marktplatz, Innsbruck city centre	9.5km		280m	1hr 15 mins–1hr 45mins	244

Mountain activities for families

Route no	Route	Start/Finish	Distance	Time	Activity	Page
55	Wusel Lake trail, Achensee	Maurach Prälatenhaus/Schwarzenau	3.8km	1–1hr 30mins	Pushchair- and cycle-friendly walk with activity stations	248
56	Ghost trail, Oberperfuss	Top station of the Rangger-Köpfl gondola, Oberperfuss/Speichersee reservoir, Rangger-Köpfl	1.6km	1hr 30mins	Hiking trail with activity stations	251
57	Scheibenweg trail	Mid-station of the Schlick 2000 ski area, Fulpmes	2km	1hr 20mins	Hiking trail with activity stations	253
58	Kugelwald Adventure World, Glungezer	Top station of the Halsmarter lift, Glungezer, Tulfes	N/a	N/a	Adventure playground and forest	255
59	Patscherkofel summit path	Top station of the Patscherkofel lift, Igls	5km	1hr 40mins	Pushchair-friendly trail	257
60	Piburgersee	Piburg	N/a	N/a	Various, including walks and swimming	259

APPENDIX B
Useful contacts

Tourist information

General information
For upcoming events and lots of useful information about Innsbruck city in English
www.innsbruck.info/en/

For a wealth of information about places to visit and things to do in Tirol, in English
www.tyrol.com

For the UK branch of the Austrian Alpine Club
www.aacuk.org.uk

Tourist information offices
Innsbruck
tel 051253 560
info@innsbruck.info

Kühtai
tel 05239 5222
www.kuehtai.info

Ötztal
tel 05253 20130
www.oetztal.at

Seefeld
tel 0508800
www.seefeld.com

Stubai
tel 0501 8810
www.stubai.at

Attractions
Innsbruck Alpine Zoo
www.alpenzoo.at

Mountain guides and equipment
There are not many guides in Innsbruck in comparison with other areas of the Alps.

For a guiding organisation
www2.bergfuehrer.at/Sektion-Innsbruck/

For private guide Stefan Rössler
www.oberhell.at/home

For equipment rentals in Innsbruck
www.dieboerse.at
www.bike-point.at
www.crazybikez.com
www.sport-gramshammer.com

Transport
For the local bus timetables
www.ivb.at

For train timetables and prices
www.oebb.at

Sports insurance
Austrian Alpine Club (UK branch)
www.aacuk.org.uk

British Mountaineering Council (BMC)
www.thebmc.co.uk

German Alpine Club
www.alpenverein.de

Snowcard
www.snowcard.co.uk

Mountain huts and restaurants

Accommodation is available at the following huts unless stated.

Aldranser Alm
Refreshments only
Open May until October, closed on Thursdays
tel 0664 1516675
www.aldranseralm.at

Alpengasthaus Stockerhof
Refreshments only
Open daily throughout the summer
tel 0664 5328806

Alpenrose Hotel, Kühtai
Open in winter only
tel 05239 5205
www.hotel-alpenrose.eu

Arzler Alm
Refreshments only
Open January until November
tel 0664 6553395
www.arzleralm.at

Bayreuther Hütte
24 bunk beds, 28 mattresses on the floor
Open from Pentecost until mid October
tel 0664 3425103
www.bayreuther-huette.de

Bettelwurfhütte
32 bunk beds, 30 mattresses on the floor
Open early June to mid October
tel 05223 53353
www.bettelwurfhuette.at

Birgitzer Alm
Refreshments only
Open May until October and December until March
tel 0664 5970026
www.birgitzer-alm.at

Birgitzkopflhaus
Open from June until October and December until April
tel 05234 68100
www.wildlife.at

Bodenstein Alm
Refreshments only
Open May until October
tel 0664 1043945

Breslauer Hütte, Ötztal
67 bunk beds, 99 mattresses on the floor
Open mid June until end of September
tel 0676 9634596
www.breslauerhuette.at

Dreiseenhütte, Kühtai
Refreshments only
Open June until September
tel 05239 5207

Elferhütte
Open June until September
tel 05226 2818
www.elferhuette.at

Franz-Senn Hütte, Stubaital
Open mid June until mid October
tel 05226 2218
www.franzsennhuette.at

Gasthof Halsmarter
Refreshments only
Open early June until early October
tel 0650 9628536
www.halsmarter.at

Gasthof Heiligwasser
Refreshments only
Open year round, closed Tuesday and Wednesday
tel 0512 377171
www.heiligwasser.at

Gasthof Zur Post, Hinterriss
Open year round
tel 05245 206
www.post-hinterriss.info

Glungezer Hütte
Open June until October and December
until April
tel 05223 78018
www.glungezer.at

Götzner Alm
Refreshments only
Open May until October
tel +53 005234/32730
www.goetzneralm.at

Graf-Ferdinand-Haus hut, Kühtai
Only open during the winter
tel 05239 21666
www.graf-ferdinand.at

Grawa Alm, Stubaital
Refreshments only
Summer opening from mid May until
end of September
tel 0676 4121009
www.feldhof-tirol.com

Hildesheimer Hütte
20 bunk beds, 56 mattresses on the
floor
Open mid/end June until mid/end
September
tel 05254 2300
www.hildesheimerhuette.at

Innsbrucker Hütte, Stubaital
30 bunk beds, 100 mattresses on the
floor
Open mid June until early October
tel 05276 295
www.innsbrucker-huette.at

Karwendelhaus
52 bunk beds, 141 mattresses on the
floor
Open early June to mid October
tel 0720 983554
www.karwendelhaus.com

Kreither Alm
Refreshments only
Open early June until mid October
tel 0677 61669613
www.kreither-alm.at

Lamsenjochhütte
22 bunk beds, 94 mattresses on the
floor
Open June until mid October
tel 05244 62063
www.lamsenjochhuette.at

Lottenseehütte
Refreshments only
Open from May until October and
December until April
tel 0664 4003132
www.lottensee.at

Maria Waldrast pilgrimage church
Open throughout the summer
tel 05273 6219
www.mariawaldrast.at

Möserer Seestuben
Refreshments only
Open throughout the summer, closed
on Mondays
tel 05212 4779
https://seestubn.webnode.at

Mutterer Alm
Refreshments only
Open year round
tel 0512 548330
www.muttereralmpark.at

Nockhof farm, Mutters
Refreshments only
Open throughout the summer
tel 0699 81371264
www.nockhof.at

Oberissalm, Oberbergtal
Currently being leased, not open to the public

Pfarrachalm
Refreshments only
Open May until September
tel 0664 3555811

Pfeishütte
30 bunk beds, 50 mattresses on the floor
Open mid June to mid October
tel 0720 316596
www.pfeishuette.at

Pinnisalm, Stubaital
Open from December to October
tel 0676 6082864

Restaurant Gipfelstube, Patscherkofel
Refreshments only
Open year round
tel 0664 9259351
www.gipfelstube.at

Rinner Alm
Refreshments only
Open year round
tel 05223 78409
www.rinner-alm.com

Rosskogel hut, Rangger Kopfl
Open July until September
tel 05232 81419
www.rosskogelhuette.tirol

Schlickeralm
Open daily throughout the summer
tel 05225 62409
www.schlickeralm.com

Sistranser Alm
Refreshments only
Open May until October, closed Mondays and Tuesdays
tel 0664 3555811
www.sistranseralm.tirol

Stablein restaurant, Ötztal
Refreshments only
tel 05254 30128

Stiglreith restaurant
Refreshments only
Open daily during the summer
tel 05232 77130

Sulzenau Alm, Stubaital
Refreshments only
Open from May until October
tel 00676 5603090
www.sulzenau-alm.at

Sulzenauhütte, Stubaital
40 bunk beds, 100 mattresses on the floor
Open early June until end of September
tel 0664 2716898
www.sulzenauhuette.at

Sulzstich restaurant
Refreshments only
Open weekends from mid June, then daily from July
tel 05232 77159

Tschangelair Alm, Stubaital
Open from mid February until December
tel 05226 3767
https://hoferwirt.at/tschangelair-alm/

Tulfein Alm
Open December to October
tel 05223 78153

Umbruggler Alm
Refreshments only
Open year round
tel 0664 3244543
www.umbrueggleralm.at

Wildmoosalm
Refreshments only
Open December until October
tel 05212 3066
www.wildmoosalm.com

Emergencies
European emergencies
tel 112

Alpine rescue
tel 140

Ambulance
tel 144

Fire brigade
tel 122

Police
tel 133

APPENDIX C
Glossary

Greetings and pleasantries

hello	hallo, guten Tag, servus, grüss Gott, grias di or grias enk (final two very Tirolean!)
goodbye	auf Wiedersehen, tschüss or pfiat di
sorry or excuse me	entschuldigung
thank you	danke or vielen Dank
have a good day	schönen Tag
please	bitte

Lifts and cable cars

cable car	die Seilbahn
chairlift	die Sesselbahn
first/last	erste/letzte
lift up/lift down	Bergstation/Talstation

Directions and navigation

where is…?	wo ist…?
straight ahead	geradeaus
left/right	links/rechts
I'm looking for…	Ich suche…
map	die Landkarte
compass	der Kompass
guidebook	das Reisebuch
north	nord
south	süd
east	ost
west	west
road/street	die Straße
path	der Weg
summit/peak	der Gipfel
river	der Fluss
stream	der Strom
bridge	die Brücke
train station	der Bahnhof

tourist information	die Touristeninformation
airport	der Flughafen

Climbing/Via ferrata equipment

via ferrata	der Klettersteig
climbing harness	der Klettergurt
rope	das Seil
lanyard	das Lanyard
carabiner	der Karabiner
helmet	der Helm

Weather

weather forecast	der Wetterbericht
hot	heiß
cold	kalt
sunny	sonnig
rainy	regnerisch
windy	windig
cloudy	bewölkt
stormy	stürmisch
temperature	die Temperatur

Emergencies

help!	zu Hilfe!
we need a helicopter	wir brauchen einen Helikopter
we need an ambulance	wir brauchen einen Krankenwagen
an accident	ein Unfall
an emergency	ein Notfall
stop!	halt!
rescue	die Rettung
helicopter	der Helikopter
ambulance	der Krankenwagen
hospital	das Krankenhaus
doctor (m/f)	der Arzt/Die Ärztin
dentist (m/f)	der Zahnarzt/Die Zahnärztin
broken arm/leg	gebrochener Arm/Bein
I am lost	ich bin verloren

Other useful words

open	geöffnet
closed	geschlossen

APPENDIX D

Index of routes by location

Brenner
Route 34 Peter Kofler klettersteig (via ferrata)

Route 43 Maria Waldrast tour (mountain biking)

Innsbruck (city and environs)
Route 1 Innsbrucker Almenweg (day walks)

Route 2 Zirbenweg (day walks)

Route 4 Dreiseen hiking trail (day walks)

Route 7 Arzler Alm (day walks)

Route 8 Aldranser Alm (day walks)

Route 9 Bodenstein Alm (day walks)

Route 10 Kreither Alm (day walks)

Route 13 Glungezer klettersteig (adventure walks and scrambles)

Route 14 Brandjochspitze (adventure walks and scrambles)

Route 16 Nordgrat Zwölferkogel (adventure walks and scrambles)

Route 18 Nordkette traverse (overnight hut walks)

Route 25 Arzbergklamm (sport climbing)

Route 26 OeAV klettergarten (sport climbing)

Route 30 Emmentaler multi-pitch (sport climbing)

Route 31 Innsbrucker klettersteig (via ferrata)

Route 37 Kühtai Panorama klettersteig (via ferrata)

Route 39 Nordkette singletrail (mountain biking)

Route 41 Rinn to Rinner Alm (mountain biking)

Route 42 Aldrans to Aldranser Alm (mountain biking)

Route 44 Mutters loop (mountain biking)

Route 46 Innsbruck loop (road cycling)

Route 47 Igls loop (road cycling)

Route 48 Innsbruck to the Mieminger Plateau (road cycling)

Route 49 Innsbruck – Telfs – Innsbruck (road cycling)

Route 50 5 Brücken Runde (city and trail running)

Route 51 Bergisel-Lauf city run (city and trail running)

Route 52 Sill-Inn-Schleife (city and trail running)

Route 53 Wolfele-Wilde-weg (city and trail running)

Route 54 Mühlau Runde (city and trail running)

Inntal (East)

Route 20 Rofan Range hike (overnight hut walks)

Route 17 Halltal hike (overnight hut walks)

Route 28 Rofan cragging, Achensee (sport climbing)

Route 32 Achensee 5 Gipfel (via ferrata)

Route 38 Absamer klettersteig (plus Westgrat and Eisengattergrat klettersteig) (via ferrata)

Route 45 Gnadenwald Plateau (road cycling)

Route 55 Wusel lake trail, Achensee (family activities)

Route 58 Kugelwald Adventure World, Glungezer (family activities)

Route 59 Patscherkofel summit path (family activities)

Inntal (West)

Route 6 Three Lakes, Seefeld Plateau (day walks)

Route 33 Crazy Eddy klettersteig (via ferrata)

Route 36 Geierwand klettersteig (via ferrata)

Route 56 Ghost trail, Oberperfuss (family activities)

Karwendel

Route 19 Karwendel traverse (overnight hut walks)

Route 40 Karwendel loop (mountain biking)

Ötztal

Route 12 Südlicher and Nordlicher Polleskogel (adventure walks and scrambles)

Route 15 Nordgrat–Vordere Sommerwand (adventure walks and scrambles)

Route 24 Wildspitze (alpine mountaineering)

Route 27 Engelswand (sport climbing)

Route 29 Klettergarten Oetz (sport climbing)

Route 60 Piburgersee (family activities)

Stubaital

LISTING OF CICERONE GUIDES

SCOTLAND

Backpacker's Britain: Northern Scotland
Ben Nevis and Glen Coe
Cycling in the Hebrides
Great Mountain Days in Scotland
Mountain Biking in Southern and Central Scotland
Mountain Biking in West and North West Scotland
Not the West Highland Way Scotland
Scotland's Best Small Mountains
Scotland's Far West
Scotland's Mountain Ridges
Scrambles in Lochaber
The Ayrshire and Arran Coastal Paths
The Border Country
The Cape Wrath Trail
The Great Glen Way
The Great Glen Way Map Booklet
The Hebridean Way
The Hebrides
The Isle of Mull
The Isle of Skye
The Skye Trail
The Southern Upland Way
The Speyside Way
The Speyside Way Map Booklet
The West Highland Way
Walking Highland Perthshire
Walking in Scotland's Far North
Walking in the Angus Glens
Walking in the Cairngorms
Walking in the Ochils, Campsie Fells and Lomond Hills
Walking in the Pentland Hills
Walking in the Southern Uplands
Walking in Torridon
Walking Loch Lomond and the Trossachs
Walking on Arran
Walking on Harris and Lewis
Walking on Jura, Islay and Colonsay
Walking on Rum and the Small Isles
Walking on the Orkney and Shetland Isles
Walking on Uist and Barra
Walking the Corbetts
  Vol 1 South of the Great Glen
Walking the Corbetts
  Vol 2 North of the Great Glen
Walking the Galloway Hills
Walking the Munros
  Vol 1 – Southern, Central and Western Highlands

Walking the Munros
  Vol 2 – Northern Highlands and the Cairngorms
West Highland Way Map Booklet
Winter Climbs Ben Nevis and Glen Coe
Winter Climbs in the Cairngorms

NORTHERN ENGLAND TRAILS

Hadrian's Wall Path
Hadrian's Wall Path Map Booklet
Pennine Way Map Booklet
The Coast to Coast Map Booklet
The Coast to Coast Walk
The Dales Way
The Dales Way Map Booklet
The Pennine Way

LAKE DISTRICT

Cycling in the Lake District
Great Mountain Days in the Lake District
Lake District Winter Climbs
Lake District: High Level and Fell Walks
Lake District: Low Level and Lake Walks
Lakeland Fellranger
Mountain Biking in the Lake District
Scrambles in the Lake District – North and South
Short Walks in Lakeland Book 1: South Lakeland
Short Walks in Lakeland Book 2: North Lakeland
Short Walks in Lakeland Book 3: West Lakeland
Tour of the Lake District
Trail and Fell Running in the Lake District

NORTH WEST ENGLAND AND THE ISLE OF MAN

Cycling the Pennine Bridleway
Cycling the Way of the Roses
Isle of Man Coastal Path
The Lancashire Cycleway
The Lune Valley and Howgills
The Ribble Way
Walking in Cumbria's Eden Valley
Walking in Lancashire
Walking in the Forest of Bowland and Pendle
Walking on the Isle of Man
Walking on the West Pennine Moors
Walks in Lancashire Witch Country
Walks in Ribble Country
Walks in Silverdale and Arnside

NORTH EAST ENGLAND, YORKSHIRE DALES AND PENNINES

Cycling in the Yorkshire Dales
Great Mountain Days in the Pennines
Mountain Biking in the Yorkshire Dales
South Pennine Walks
St Oswald's Way and St Cuthbert's Way
The Cleveland Way and the Yorkshire Wolds Way
The Cleveland Way Map Booklet
The North York Moors
The Reivers Way
The Teesdale Way
Walking in County Durham
Walking in Northumberland
Walking in the North Pennines
Walking in the Yorkshire Dales: North and East
Walking in the Yorkshire Dales: South and West
Walks in Dales Country
Walks in the Yorkshire Dales

WALES AND WELSH BORDERS

Glyndwr's Way
Great Mountain Days in Snowdonia
Hillwalking in Shropshire
Hillwalking in Wales – Vol 1
Hillwalking in Wales – Vol 2
Mountain Walking in Snowdonia
Offa's Dyke Path
Offa's Dyke Map Booklet
Pembrokeshire Coast Path Map Booklet
Ridges of Snowdonia
Scrambles in Snowdonia
The Ascent of Snowdon
The Ceredigion and Snowdonia Coast Paths
The Pembrokeshire Coast Path
The Severn Way
The Snowdonia Way
The Wales Coast Path
The Wye Valley Walk
Walking in Carmarthenshire
Walking in Pembrokeshire
Walking in the Forest of Dean
Walking in the South Wales Valleys
Walking in the Wye Valley
Walking on the Brecon Beacons
Walking on the Gower
Welsh Winter Climbs

IRELAND

The Irish Coast to Coast Walk
The Mountains of Ireland
The Wild Atlantic Way and
Western Ireland

ITALY

Italy's Sibillini National Park
Shorter Walks in the Dolomites
Ski Touring and Snowshoeing in the
Dolomites
The Way of St Francis
Through the Italian Alps
Trekking in the Apennines
Trekking in the Dolomites
Via Ferratas of the Italian Dolomites
Vol 1
Via Ferratas of the Italian
Dolomites: Vol 2
Walking and Trekking in the Gran
Paradiso
Walking in Abruzzo
Walking in Italy's Stelvio National
Park
Walking in Sardinia
Walking in Sicily
Walking in the Dolomites
Walking in Tuscany
Walking in Umbria
Walking on the Amalfi Coast
Walking the Italian Lakes
Walks and Treks in the Maritime
Alps

SCANDINAVIA: NORWAY, SWEDEN, FINLAND

Walking in Norway

EASTERN EUROPE AND THE BALKANS

The Danube Cycleway Volume 2
The High Tatras
The Mountains of Romania
Walking in Bulgaria's National
Parks
Walking in Hungary
Mountain Biking in Slovenia
The Islands of Croatia
The Julian Alps of Slovenia
The Mountains of Montenegro
The Peaks of the Balkans Trail
Trekking in Slovenia
Walking in Croatia
Walking in Slovenia: The
Karavanke

SPAIN

Coastal Walks in Andalucia
Cycle Touring in Spain
Mountain Walking in Mallorca
Mountain Walking in Southern
Catalunya
Spain's Sendero Histórico: The GR1
The Andalucian Coast to Coast
Walk
The Mountains of Nerja
The Mountains of Ronda and
Grazalema
The Northern Caminos
The Sierras of Extremadura
The Way of St James Cyclist Guide
Trekking in Mallorca
Walking and Trekking in the Sierra
Nevada
Walking in Andalucia
Walking in Menorca
Walking in the Cordillera
Cantabrica
Walking on Gran Canaria
Walking on La Gomera and El
Hierro
Walking on La Palma
Walking on Lanzarote and
Fuerteventura
Walking on Tenerife
Walking on the Costa Blanca

PORTUGAL

The Camino Portugués
Walking in Portugal
Walking in the Algarve

GREECE, CYPRUS AND MALTA

The High Mountains of Crete
Trekking in Greece
Walking and Trekking on Corfu
Walking in Cyprus
Walking on Malta

INTERNATIONAL CHALLENGES, COLLECTIONS AND ACTIVITIES

Canyoning in the Alps
The Via Francigena Canterbury to
Rome – Parts 1 and 2

AFRICA

Climbing in the Moroccan Anti-
Atlas
Mountaineering in the Moroccan
High Atlas
The High Atlas
Trekking in the Atlas Mountains
Kilimanjaro
Walking in the Drakensberg

JORDAN

Jordan – Walks, Treks, Caves,
Climbs and Canyons
Treks and Climbs in Wadi Rum,
Jordan

ASIA

Annapurna
Everest: A Trekker's Guide
Trekking in the Himalaya
Trekking in Bhutan
Trekking in Ladakh
The Mount Kailash Trek

USA AND CANADA

British Columbia
The John Muir Trail
The Pacific Crest Trail

ARGENTINA, CHILE AND PERU

Aconcagua and the Southern Andes
Hiking and Biking Peru's Inca Trails
Torres del Paine

TECHNIQUES

Geocaching in the UK
Indoor Climbing
Lightweight Camping
Map and Compass
Outdoor Photography
Polar Exploration
Rock Climbing
Sport Climbing
The Mountain Hut Book

MINI GUIDES

Alpine Flowers
Avalanche!
Navigation
Pocket First Aid and Wilderness
Medicine
Snow

MOUNTAIN LITERATURE

8000 metres
A Walk in the Clouds
Abode of the Gods
The Pennine Way – the Path, the
People, the Journey
Unjustifiable Risk?

For full information on all our
guides, books and eBooks,
visit our website:
www.cicerone.co.uk

Walking – Trekking – Mountaineering – Climbing – Cycling

Over 40 years, Cicerone have built up an outstanding collection of over 300 guides, inspiring all sorts of amazing adventures.

Every guide comes from extensive exploration and research by our expert authors, all with a passion for their subjects. They are frequently praised, endorsed and used by clubs, instructors and outdoor organisations.

All our titles can now be bought as **e-books**, **ePubs** and **Kindle** files and we also have an online magazine – **Cicerone Extra** – with features to help cyclists, climbers, walkers and trekkers choose their next adventure, at home or abroad.

Our website shows any **new information** we've had in since a book was published. Please do let us know if you find anything has changed, so that we can publish the latest details. On our **website** you'll also find great ideas and lots of detailed information about what's inside every guide and you can buy **individual routes** from many of them online.

It's easy to keep in touch with what's going on at Cicerone by getting our monthly **free e-newsletter**, which is full of offers, competitions, up-to-date information and topical articles. You can subscribe on our home page and also follow us on **Facebook** and **Twitter** or dip into our **blog**.

Cicerone – the very best guides for exploring the world.

CICERONE

Juniper House, Murley Moss, Oxenholme Road, Kendal, Cumbria LA9 7RL
Tel: 015395 62069 info@cicerone.co.uk
www.cicerone.co.uk